THE BEDFORD SERIES IN HISTORY AND CULTURE

# Spartacus and the Slave Wars

## A Brief History with Documents

### SECOND EDITION

## Brent D. Shaw

*Princeton University*

D0595526

bedford/st.martin's
Macmillan Learning
Boston | New York

*For Bedford/St. Martin's*

*Vice President, Editorial, Macmillan Learning Humanities*: Edwin Hill
*Program Director for History*: Michael Rosenberg
*Senior Program Manager for History*: Laura Arcari
*History Marketing Manager*: Melissa Rodriguez
*Director of Content Development*: Jane Knetzger
*Associate Editor*: Mary Posman Starowicz
*Assistant Editor*: Melanie McFadyen
*Content Project Manager*: Lidia MacDonald-Carr
*Workflow Supervisor*: Joe Ford
*Production Supervisor*: Robin Besofsky
*Media Project Manager*: Michelle Camisa
*Manager of Publishing Services*: Andrea Cava
*Project Management*: Lumina Datamatics, Inc.
*Composition*: Lumina Datamatics, Inc.
*Cartographer*: Mapping Specialists, Ltd.
*Director of Rights and Permissions*: Hilary Newman
*Permissions Manager*: Kalina Inghman
*Senior Art Director*: Anna Palchik
*Cover Design*: William Boardman
*Cover Photo*: Relief depicting games at the Circus Maximus (stone)/ Roman, (1st century
    AD)/ Museo della Civilta Romana, Rome, Italy/Bridgeman Images
*Printing and Binding*: LSC Communications

Copyright © 2018, 2001 by Bedford/St. Martin's.

All rights reserved. No part of this book may be reproduced, stored in a retrieval system,
or transmitted in any form or by any means, electronic, mechanical, photocopying,
recording, or otherwise, except as may be expressly permitted by the applicable
copyright statutes or in writing by the Publisher.

Manufactured in the United States of America.

2   1   0   9   8   7
f   e   d   c   b   a

*For information, write*: Bedford/St. Martin's, 75 Arlington Street, Boston, MA 02116

ISBN: 978-1-319-09482-9

**Acknowledgments**
*Acknowledgments and copyrights appear on the same page as the text and art selections they
cover; these acknowledgments and copyrights constitute an extension of the copyright page.*

At the time of publication all Internet URLs published in this text were found to
accurately link to their intended website. If you do find a broken link, please forward the
information to history@macmillan.com so that it can be corrected for the next printing.

# Foreword

The Bedford Series in History and Culture is designed so that readers can study the past as historians do.

The historian's first task is finding the evidence. Documents, letters, memoirs, interviews, pictures, movies, novels, or poems can provide facts and clues. Then the historian questions and compares the sources. There is more to do than in a courtroom, for hearsay evidence is welcome, and the historian is usually looking for answers beyond act and motive. Different views of an event may be as important as a single verdict. How a story is told may yield as much information as what it says.

Along the way the historian seeks help from other historians and perhaps from specialists in other disciplines. Finally, it is time to write, to decide on an interpretation and how to arrange the evidence for readers.

Each book in this series contains an important historical document or group of documents, each document a witness from the past and open to interpretation in different ways. The documents are combined with some element of historical narrative—an introduction or a biographical essay, for example—that provides students with an analysis of the primary source material and important background information about the world in which it was produced.

Each book in the series focuses on a specific topic within a specific historical period. Each provides a basis for lively thought and discussion about several aspects of the topic and the historian's role. Each is short enough (and inexpensive enough) to be a reasonable one-week assignment in a college course. Whether as classroom or personal reading, each book in the series provides firsthand experience of the challenge—and fun—of discovering, recreating, and interpreting the past.

Lynn Hunt
David W. Blight
Bonnie G. Smith

# Preface

In 73 B.C.E., in the heart of Italy, at the very center of Rome's Mediterranean empire, a slave named Spartacus led a breakout from the prison-like conditions in which gladiators like himself were trained for the murderous and popular entertainments staged for avid spectators. He ignited one of the most violent episodes of slave resistance known in the history of the Roman Empire—indeed, in the world annals of slavery. It is a paradox of sorts that this event, so important to the history of slavery, is so well known in general but so badly documented in particular. Our ignorance is not just a question of the poor state of the historical evidence. It has also been encouraged by the portrayal of Spartacus and his followers in modern stage plays, novels, and films as epic lonely individuals who acted in a heroic fashion to strike out for freedom, against all odds and reason. Part of the aim of this book is to restore some of the larger context of slave resistance in the Roman Empire within which the actions of Spartacus and his followers can be better understood. By restoring some of this history, I hope that readers will find more than just a daring individual fronting a spectacular armed rebellion.

The new edition of *Spartacus and the Slave Wars*, composed a decade and a half after the first version, offers a welcome opportunity for revision, correction, and addition. At the end of my original introductory essay, for example, I had the temerity to suggest that the image of Spartacus as a symbol of liberty had come to an end. I was perhaps too hasty. I think it would have been more accurate to say that that particular image of Spartacus appears to have ended. But an ongoing fascination with the man and his achievements in fictional replayings in film and television has not subsided. The new Spartacus seems to be less the old romantic political liberal or rebel and more part of a subversive cultural moment hinted at in the revised introduction. Spartacus does indeed seem to have new life in him.

The primary sources in Part Two were selected to provide readers with some basic background information on slavery in the ancient world. They include translations of original Greek and Latin writings not only on the lives and deaths of gladiators but also on the routines of the far more numerous slaves who worked on the farms of Italy and Sicily. They also highlight the ways in which some of these slaves resisted their enforced work regimens. The readings are designed to draw attention to the means short of mass armed rebellion that slaves used to free themselves from the constraints of servitude, especially the effective stratagem of simply running away. More directly relevant to understanding the emergence of armed slave resistance on the scale of regular wars are the records of the two slave wars in the Roman province of Sicily (135–132 B.C.E. and 104–100 B.C.E.) that preceded the Spartacus war. Given the modern-day fascination with Spartacus and the forces that he led, it is perhaps ironic that these earlier, less well-known (but better documented) wars offer more coherent pictures of the outbreak, course, and repression of slave wars in the late Roman Republic. The records that survive about the Sicilian slave wars not only provide essential background information for the Spartacus war but also are highly significant events in Roman slave history.

I have added a few more documents to the collection for the new edition, deleted some redundant ones, and corrected and revised the existing translations. I have also added new headnotes to the documents to aid student analysis. Particularly in the case of the fragments from Sallust's *Histories* I have been able to consult and to benefit from John T. Ramsey's volume on the fragments of Sallust's *Histories* that appeared in the Loeb Classical Library in 2015. More specific reading suggestions are included in the Selected Bibliography, which has also been fully revised. Other pedagogical aids include the Chronology, the Glossary of Greek and Latin Terms, and a revised set of Questions for Consideration.

The great caveat issued to both teacher and student alike is that the history of slave resistance and war in the Roman Republic is badly fragmented. Many of the firsthand sources have not survived intact, and even those that have survived or have been assiduously pieced together by modern scholars are not easy to translate into current English. Both the piecemeal nature of the original Greek and Latin texts and the alien nature of social and political institutions of a society that flourished more than two thousand years ago conspire to make any transcription of these texts a difficult task. I have attempted to give as much general background and guidance as space allows, and I firmly urge students to read this book in order, beginning with the introduction in Part One, advancing to the better-documented Sicilian slave wars, and finally proceeding on to the Spartacus war in Part Two.

Only by viewing Spartacus as part of the more general forces at work in Italy and Sicily during the second and first centuries B.C.E. can we understand his role in particular, and that of slaves in general, in the history of the Roman Republic.

## A NOTE ABOUT THE TEXT

When you read these documents, it is important to be aware of the nature of the sources in which the information appears. To that end, I have provided a general description of the most important authors of the literary works from which this information has been derived ("List of the Principal Authors and Literary Sources"). The dates provided for many of these authors are approximate, not much better than educated guesswork.

I selected the texts, including the specific parts and fragments of them, that I deemed to be most useful and accessible. Where there has been much scholarly dispute about fragmentary texts and the ordering of fragments, I tended to follow the standard editions. I translated all the texts myself, but naturally I consulted existing translations. On occasion, I could not find a better turn of phrase or choice of words, and so I note here my gratitude to my predecessors.

In accordance with the general practice of this series, a date is provided in the heading that indicates the general date of the source or writer of that document. For example, when Document 37 by the historian Appian notes "Second Century C.E.," it is indicating the general era in which Appian wrote and *not* the dates of the events themselves (in this case, 133 B.C.E). Similarly, when Document 41 by Valerius Maximus notes "First Century C.E.," it is indicating the general age when Valerius Maximus wrote and *not* the date of the events in the document (which date to the 130s B.C.E.). The student should be aware of this distinction.

## ACKNOWLEDGMENTS

Even in small works, the accumulation of personal debt is great. I thank those who provided critical readings of the first edition of the text: Ernst Badian, Harvard University; Keith Bradley, University of Notre Dame; T. Corey Brennan, Rutgers University; Bruce Frier, University of Michigan; Ron Mellor, University of California Los Angeles; Richard Saller, Stanford University; and Valerie Warrior, credit for whose critical comments was inadvertently overlooked in the first edition—I am happy to correct the oversight here.

A more personal note of thanks is offered to Howard Fast for answering some questions and a request by mail; and to my former graduate student Alex Thein for providing assistance in checking some of the translations. I owe a special personal debt to my friend Henry MacAdam for numerous entertaining bits of repartee on matters Spartacan—from Rosa Luxemburg and Arthur Koestler to Hollywood and beyond—and also for the loan of his fascinating correspondence on Spartacus with Kirk Douglas. My gratitude also goes to Marcia Tucker, librarian of the Institute for Advanced Study (IAS) in Princeton, New Jersey, and to Karen Downing, photographic technician, also of the IAS, for their assistance in helping to produce the illustrations for the first edition.

My special thanks go to Molly Kalkstein, who was not just the editor of the first edition but also a model of patience and forbearance. Her careful eye, her attention to detail and the larger purpose, and her encouragement and help in matters large and small were necessary to the completion of the work. She is perhaps only to be exceeded by that very model of patience, Shauna, who read and reread drafts of the translations, the introduction, and attendant materials, and who had the energy to persist. *Sine quibus*, as they say.

Of those who gave assistance for this revision, I must thank, once again, my friend Dr. Henry MacAdam, who both discussed many of the details and drew my attention to new materials relevant to the project. Finally, I must especially thank my front-line helpers at Bedford/St. Martin's: Program Director Michael Rosenberg, Senior Program Manager Laura Arcari, History Marketing Manager Melissa Rodriguez, Assistant Editor Melanie McFadyen, Associate Editor Mary Posman Starowicz, Cover Designer William Boardman, and Content Project Manager Lidia MacDonald-Carr. As I said before, the old adage "without whom" applies very strongly to them. Finally, it is surely true (as Lynn Hunt has also remarked) that I have learned as many important things from my students over the last decades of teaching as anything that I have taught them. It is especially fitting that I dedicate this book to them.

Brent D. Shaw

# Contents

# Maps and Illustrations

# PART ONE

# Introduction:
# The Roman Slave Wars
# and History

In the midsummer of 73 B.C.E., a savage uprising of rebel slaves erupted and then raged throughout Italy for the next two years. According to some stories, the violence was sparked by the escape of seventy slaves from a gladiatorial training school in the luxurious city of Capua, about 125 miles south of Rome. Whatever its precise origins, the slave revolt soon escalated into a larger-scale conflict, a war in which tens of thousands of slaves joined in mass armed resistance against their owners. Their main aim was, quite simply, to free themselves from the conditions of servitude in which they were forced to live. Whether the brutalities of this war were worse than the savageries of the civil war that the Romans had suffered in the previous decade is difficult to say. But the violence of this conflict, which pitted slaves against both their masters and the armed forces of the Roman state, was nevertheless particularly brutal. The battles, ambushes, and armed skirmishes that the slaves fought constitute one of the greatest wars of resistance in the history of slavery and the most famous slave war in ancient history. But it was actually the last in a series of three great slave rebellions that beleaguered Rome between the mid-130s and the late 70s B.C.E.

The two earlier slave wars were centered farther south, on the island of Sicily, the first of the Roman Empire's overseas provinces. The first Sicilian slave war lasted from 135 to 132 B.C.E.; the second raged from 104 to 100 B.C.E.[1] Two charismatic slave commanders led the forces in each war: Eunus and Kleon in the first and Athenion and Salvius in the second.

1

The last of the three great slave wars was fought mainly in southern Italy between 73 and 71 B.C.E. Although Spartacus emerged as the principal leader of this war, he was only one of many slaves involved in the incident that sparked the war. Who was Spartacus? Today he is a symbol of resistance to domination of mythic proportions, best known to most Americans from Howard Fast's 1951 novel *Spartacus* and the 1960 film based on that book. In fact, he has become such a powerful image that to ask the question "Who was he?" only provokes more difficult questions about the origins of the slave wars of the late Roman Republic, the veils of myth and legend that have grown up around him, and the sources that survive to tell his story.

## THE SLAVE WARS IN ITALY AND SICILY

Finding out about Spartacus is more difficult than understanding his role as a modern-day symbol of resistance. To see through the masks of our own modern images of him requires us to discover who Spartacus was in the world in which he and his fellow slaves lived. Most important is for us to understand the new slave economy and society that emerged in the third and second centuries B.C.E. Once we delve into this historical context, we can begin to learn more about the daily experiences of slaves in Roman society and their limited ability to resist the slave system. By attempting to understand the constraints on large-scale resistance, we can begin to appreciate the rarity of large-scale slave rebellions not just in the Roman Empire but throughout the world.

Let us begin with the social institution of slavery in which people like Spartacus found themselves. Spartacus came from the distant land of Thrace—roughly speaking, the area of the extreme northeastern part of modern-day Greece, southeastern Bulgaria, and the small part of Turkey west of the Bosporus (Map 1). He had been sent to Italy as a prisoner to be sold as a slave. His wife, we are told, also was Thracian. It is not surprising that we do not know her name. Such was the fate of most women in ancient Greece and Rome, even those who were not slaves. (Howard Fast invented the young and beautiful Varinia, who served as the 1950s-type love interest of the book's and the film's protagonist.)

The large-scale use of slaves in Roman society came about partly because of internal economic forces and demands. Slaves also were preferred as a source of labor because of the tremendous external advantages that the Roman state reaped from its conquest of the

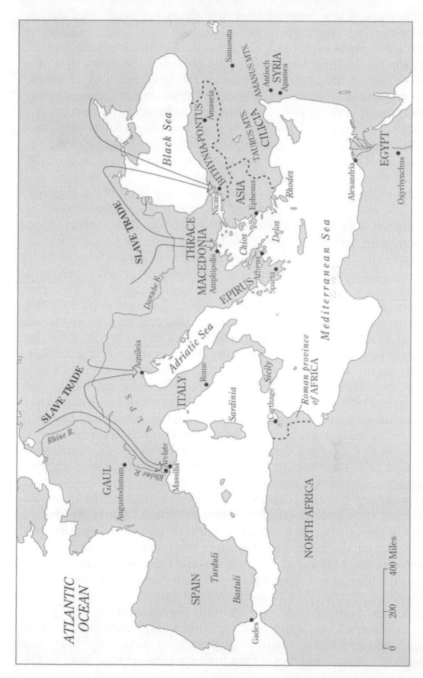

**Map 1.** *The Mediterranean World at the Time of the Slave Wars, ca. 135–70 B.C.E.*

3

Mediterranean in a series of wars that eliminated most of its serious competitors for power by the mid-second century B.C.E. The influx of wealth that resulted from these conquests and the internal demands for larger-scale agricultural production provoked the emergence of a new entrepreneurial economy based on the labor provided by slaves. The great wealth derived from Rome's Mediterranean conquests was concentrated in the hands of a relatively small number of Romans and Italians, who expended it on luxury goods and, most important, large amounts of land. To provide the labor necessary to work their new properties, landowners acquired human beings, who were bought and sold like chattels, or pieces of movable property.

The political, cultural, and economic forces that propelled this new agricultural economy also provoked the most intensive development of agrarian slavery known in the ancient world. The most extreme form of this slave agriculture was located at the very heart of the Roman Empire—in the southern parts of the Italian peninsula, especially in the region of Campania, and also on the island of Sicily, where southern Italian and Campanian interests were pervasive (Maps 2–4).[2] The same process began in the areas of North Africa that were under the control of the great city-state of Carthage, until its destruction by the Romans in 146 B.C.E.[3] In this sense, the geopolitical shape of the Roman slave system was opposite that of the system developed by the European colonial powers in the sixteenth century and later. It was not a system in which slaves from foreign lands were transported to developing lands on the frontiers or peripheries of distant overseas empires.[4] Instead, in the case of Roman Italy, slaves were imported in huge numbers into the very heart of the conquering state and transformed its basic economy.

Because of the rapid expansion of the new slave-run agriculture in the first half of the second century B.C.E., historians believe that the majority of agricultural slaves had been enslaved in their own lifetimes. Many of them had been captured in the eastern Mediterranean, where the main slave merchants and suppliers took advantage of the chaotic political conditions in the region. Whatever these slaves' specific ethnic backgrounds, the Romans tended to call them "Syrians," an ethnic stereotype used to label all "inferior persons" from the eastern Mediterranean.[5] Other slaves came from the densely populated but materially impoverished area north of the Rhine and Danube Rivers in western Europe and from the regions north of the lower Danube and the Black Sea in eastern Europe and western Eurasia. The main slave trading routes for human merchandise from the region north of the Black Sea (roughly, modern-day Ukraine) ran through Thrace to the ports on the

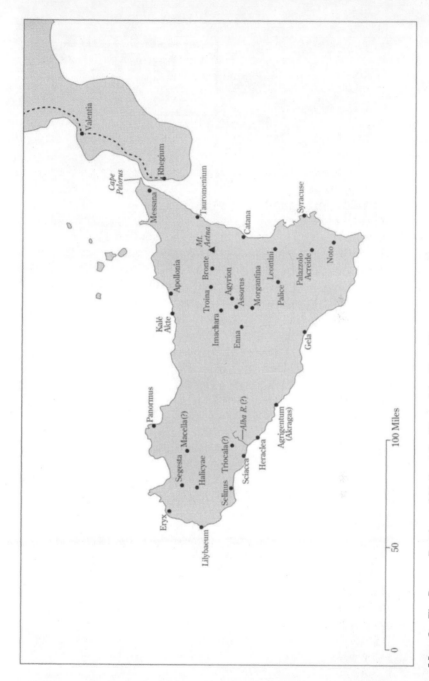

**Map 2.** *The Roman Province of Sicily at the Time of the Slave Wars, ca. 135–100 B.C.E.*

Valentia

Rhegium

Cape
Pelorus

Messana

Tauromenium

Mt.
Aetna

Catana

Syracuse

Apollonia

Bronte

Troina

Agyrion

Leontini

Noto

Palazzolo
Acreide

Imachara

Assorus

Morgantina

Kalê
Akte

Enna

Palice

Gela

Panormus

Segesta

Macella(?)

Halicyae

Triocala(?)

Alba R.(?)

Selinus

Sciacca

Agrigentum
(Akragas)

Heraclea

Eryx

Lilybaeum

0        50        100 Miles

5

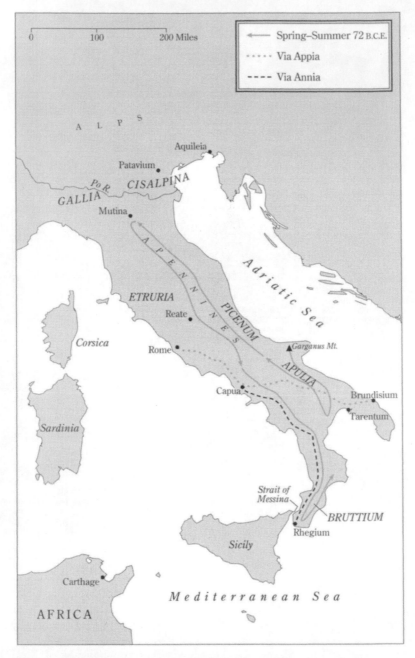

**Map 3.** *Roman Italy at the Time of the Spartacus Slave War, 73–71 B.C.E.*

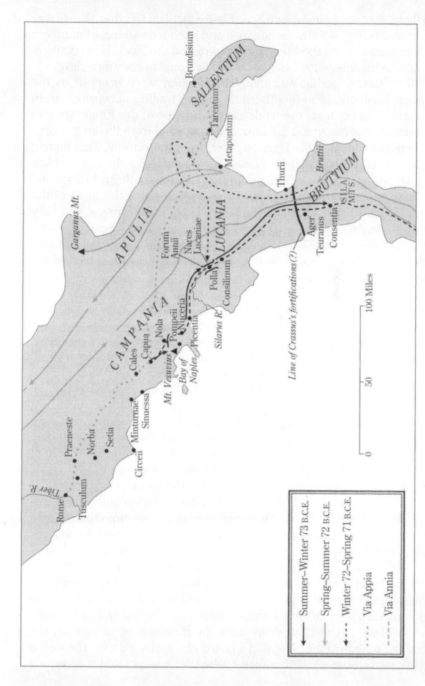

**Map 4.** *Central and Southern Italy at the Time of the Spartacus Slave War, 73–71 B.C.E.*

7

northern shores of the Aegean Sea (Figure 2).[6] The fact that Thrace was a crossroads in this traffic in humans, and itself fed significant numbers of its population into the Mediterranean region as slaves, is particularly significant in understanding Spartacus's personal history as a slave.

Other slaves, perhaps as many in number, were brought to the western Mediterranean by other major slave trading networks—from northern Europe, from the lands north and east of the Rhine River in present-day Germany and the Low Countries, and from the areas north of the upper course of the Danube River in central Europe. This human commerce came to the Mediterranean down the Rhone River to Arelate (Arles), Massilia (Marseille), and other ports in southern France and by more easterly routes to ports such as Aquileia at the head of the Adriatic Sea. These slaves were mainly Gauls and Germans, and they were ethnically distinct in language and culture from the slaves who were captured from the Scythian lands of the Black Sea. All of these major ethnic groups could be found among the slaves involved in the insurrection led by Spartacus.

A large proportion of the slaves acquired by the owners of the farms and ranches of Sicily in the first half of the second century B.C.E. came from the eastern Mediterranean. This was a direct result of Rome's military intervention in that region, mainly in the decades after 200 B.C.E. Roman expansion there entailed the military destruction and political destabilization of the Seleucid monarchy, which had ruled over the former Persian Empire following its defeat by Alexander the Great in the 330s B.C.E. The kings of Syria, such as Antiochus III and Antiochus IV, bore the brunt of Roman hegemony; their weak successors fared even worse. In the extreme political instability that followed, freebooting agents of violence on the high seas, mainly pirates from the region of Cilicia in southeastern Turkey (Map 1), became involved in large-scale raiding and kidnapping operations in which they preyed on coastal and other communities. The Cilicians became the main freelance slave suppliers of the period.[7] They even staged predatory raids into the western Mediterranean, where they were reputed to be in contact with various insurgent movements, including those led by the Roman political rebel Sertorius in Spain and the slave leader Spartacus in Italy.

In the 70s and 60s B.C.E., the pirates grew into an independent force in the Mediterranean. They were perceived as a substantial threat to the Roman state in the years immediately following the defeat of Spartacus in 71 B.C.E. Only four years later, the Roman general Pompey the Great, who had claimed the lion's share of the rewards for the defeat of Spartacus, squelched this threat when he was granted a sweeping military command by the Roman people to rid the Mediterranean of the pirate menace.

Those enslaved in the eastern Mediterranean during this period shared common linguistic, cultural, and religious backgrounds. Moreover, since many of them had not been born into slavery, they also shared the memory of freedom. These factors contributed to their willingness to communicate with each other and to entertain the possibility of armed resistance to enslavement. Some of these slaves looked to legitimate freeborn rulers as examples. Eunus, one of the leaders of the first Sicilian slave war, renamed himself King Antiochus, a name used by kings of the Seleucid monarchy in Syria, from which Eunus and many of his fellow slaves had come.[8]

Most of the slaves sold to Italian and Roman owners at this time were used as manual laborers, the majority of them in various types of agricultural work. They were the permanent workforce of a revolutionary new rural economy of plantation agriculture. Roman writers later invented the term *latifundia*, or "wide fields" (see glossary), to evoke the panoramic perspective furnished by the ownership of extensive, often widely scattered, tracts of land and of the hundreds, sometimes thousands, of slaves needed to work them. The new latifundist agriculture was oriented toward the production of marketable surpluses needed to sustain the new luxurious lifestyles demanded by Roman and Italian aristocrats, including those of the competitive political elite in the city of Rome and of wealthy men of power in the cities of southern Italy (such as Capua and Pompeii) and Sicily.[9]

Broadly speaking, the slaves who labored on these new latifundia were of two types. The first type were slaves who cultivated cereal grains, vines, olives, and other arboreal crops. Ideally, these slaves worked under close supervision. For purposes of surveillance and security, during the night or at times when they were not working, the slaves were kept penned in quarters that the Romans called *ergastula*, or "work barracks." Such slaves were often found on small but intensively worked farms in rich agricultural areas, such as those around the city of Pompeii in Campania.

The open expanses of southern Italy and Sicily were more arid and could not easily sustain a viable market-oriented agriculture based on the intensive cultivation of cash crops. In these regions, therefore, slave owners developed a different type of agriculture that mixed the cultivation of cereal crops with the raising of large herds of cattle and sheep, and sometimes pigs and goats, which were often driven over long distances to widely separated pastures. These animals spent the summer in the mountains and the winter on the lowland plains. Thus, the second type of slaves were *pastores*, or "herdsmen," who drove these animals to pasture and tended them throughout the year, and who worked under the supervision of a *magister pecoris*, or "herd master." The slaves who worked on these ranches were fundamentally different from the slaves who worked on the agricultural latifundia.[10] Slave shepherds and herders could not be constrained by chains or housed in barracks each night. They had to be free to follow the herds. In addition, they had to be armed to protect the animals from predators, rustlers, and bandits. These two factors—freedom of movement and the possession of arms—made them potentially very dangerous men.

Just as important as the two basic types of slave laborers were the elite slaves, who provided the managerial skills and technical knowledge needed to run the slave farms and ranches. These slaves made sure that the complex farming operations were carried out to the owner's satisfaction. The most important of these slaves was the *vilicus*, the "farm manager" or "bailiff," who organized the finances of the farm, bought and sold materials, and supervised the annual cycle of work. He also set the work details, controlled the workforce, and maintained surveillance over the slaves who did the manual labor.[11] These men were of great significance in the organization of any collective resistance by the slaves. Since they already had experience in controlling and directing the work and behavior of the slaves, they could easily apply the same skills to leading rebel armies and to governing new communities founded by the slaves.

The sudden introduction of a large number of slaves into a rapidly transforming economy produced conditions favorable to large-scale armed resistance against the slave owners. Three of the great slave wars washed over southern Italy and Sicily between 140 and 70 B.C.E. They occurred at approximately thirty-year intervals and so seem to reflect the similar reactions of three generations of slaves caught up in an economic revolution that depended on slave labor. The first two slave wars broke out on the island of Sicily and were confined to that island. Sicily was the site of the most rapid and intense development of slave agriculture in the first half-century after 200 B.C.E., following the second great war between Rome and its principal military and political rival in the western Mediterranean, the city-state of Carthage in North Africa. Therefore, it is not surprising that these slave wars occurred there.

The first great slave war broke out in the mid-130s B.C.E. and ended in 132 B.C.E. It was divided into two theaters of operation, western and eastern, which reflected the basic geopolitical division of Sicily. One Roman treasury official, or *quaestor* (see glossary), was in charge of the western part of the island, headquartered at Lilybaeum, and another was stationed at Syracuse, on the east coast. Slave pastoralists and herders dominated the western region, and agricultural slaves dominated the grain-producing plains of the east.

The slaves in the eastern and western parts of the island appear to have risen separately—those in the east under a slave named Eunus and those in the west under a vilicus named Kleon. Eunus was a millenarian[12] magician, a wonder-worker, and a powerful religious leader. Kleon was not only the manager of a farming operation in western Sicily, but, like Eunus, he was also reputed to possess religious powers, including the ability to utter prophesies based on his astrological skills.

The slave war gathered momentum when these two leaders and their followers combined to form a single coherent force. The rapid escalation of their strength seems to have been abetted by the slave owners themselves, who had encouraged violent behavior by allowing their slave shepherds to feed and clothe themselves by stealing what they needed from other people on the island. In addition, the response of the local authorities in Sicily was lethargic, apparently because they greatly underestimated the slaves' ability to organize a large-scale military campaign. The senate in Rome also failed to respond quickly to the threat of the armed slaves. This is explained in part by the complex nature of the Roman government, which relied on officials who served for only one year at a time.

In terms of military operations, such as those required against the insurgent slaves, the most important officials were the two *consuls* (holding powers like those of a prime minister and a military field marshal combined; see glossary) and, beneath them, the six *praetors* (the chief legal and administrative officers of the Roman state; see glossary). These high-ranking officials were usually put in charge of Roman armies that battled formidable foreign enemies. Repressing rebellious slaves was beneath the dignity of these men and the legionary soldiers they commanded. Such a sordid task was normally left to the slave owners or to local militias, which were often corrupt, weak, and provisional. As the permanent governing body of the Roman state, the senate did have a long-term perspective on events, but it had to be moved by the recognition of a manifest threat of major proportions for it to direct the consuls or praetors to use the Roman army to deal with a slave uprising.

Roman provincial governors, such as those who administered the province of Sicily, were normally former praetors (occasionally consuls), who usually held their provincial commands for one-year terms. Because they were temporary and were severely understaffed by modern standards, these governors were dependent on the wealthy and powerful men who ran local towns and cities to help them administer their provinces. These provincial elites often gave their own interests priority over the rule of law and order that was supposed to be enforced by the governors.

Given the failure of the local forces to deal with the slave uprising in Sicily, the senate finally decided to dispatch Roman army units under high-ranking commanders to the island. As a result, the first slave war was finally brought to an end.

To a considerable extent, the second great slave war, which erupted on Sicily in 104 B.C.E. and ended four years later, repeated the patterns of the first. Resistance in the eastern part of the island was led by Salvius, and resistance in the west was organized by Athenion. Despite the lesson of the first slave war, the response by the Roman senate was similarly slow. Their inadequate reaction, due in part to the need for Roman forces to face German invaders threatening northern Italy, allowed the slaves to acquire considerable momentum in the early stages of the rebellion and then to coalesce in numbers that overwhelmed the local forces trying to subdue them. Once again, only the intervention of the larger, better-trained legionary forces of the Roman army finally brought the second war to an end.

The third great slave war that threatened Italy and Sicily between 140 and 70 B.C.E. was to be the last great slave war of antiquity. The war broke out a generation after the second slave war and lasted from 73 to 71 B.C.E. It is important to note that this rebellion, led by Spartacus, differed from the first two slave wars both in location—it was centered in southern Italy rather than in Sicily—and in the nature of its leadership. The core group of slaves who incited and led the rebellion were not agricultural slaves but rather men trained to kill each other for the entertainment of others. They were known as *gladiatores*, or "men of the sword (Figure 1)."[13] Like the two earlier wars, however, most of the slaves who joined the third rebellion were simple agricultural laborers.

## SPARTACUS: THE MAN, THE MYTH, AND THE MODERN SYMBOL OF REBELLION

On April Fool's Day of 1865, Karl Marx's elder daughter, Jenny, presented her father with a playful questionnaire. Not unlike the marketing surveys of our own day, it asked questions about his likes and dislikes: the qualities that he most preferred in a person, his favorite food (fish),

**Figure 1.** *Spartacus the Gladiator*

This fresco from an entranceway to a house in Pompeii features two horse-mounted gladiators fighting each other. Compare the trumpeter to the right of the two men with the graffito of another gladiatorial contest at Pompeii (Figure 3). The captions above the men are written in Oscan, a common language in this region of southern Italy before the Roman conquest gradually shifted the common language to Latin. The caption above the rider on the left (the Oscan writing has to be read right to left) says "Lucky is [. . .] ans! (PHILI[CS] . . . ANS)" *[only the last three letters of the man's name survive]*. More important is the inscription above the mounted man to the right: "Spartacus" [SPARTAKS]. The context of the find and the use of Oscan for the captions both argue for a date of 100–70 B.C.E. This is the same period when Spartacus was in training as a gladiator. Since Spartacus is a Thracian name that was not usually found in the region of Capua and Pompeii, the coincidences of time and place have suggested the possibility of an identification with the rebel slave. This is one of the earliest wall drawings known from Pompeii.

his favorite color (not surprisingly, red), and various other preferences. The survey also asked about his hero, to which Marx replied, "Spartacus and Kepler."[14] The fact that Marx chose Spartacus suggests how well known the story of a single slave who had led tens of thousands of his fellow slaves in a war against their Roman masters had become by the mid-nineteenth century. It is rather surprising to note, therefore, that only a century earlier Spartacus was all but unknown, even to most well-educated people.

Marx's attention had been drawn to Spartacus by two significant events of his own time. First, there were the revolutionary feats of Giuseppe Garibaldi, the romantic nineteenth-century rebel who was engaged in liberating Sicily and southern Italy from foreign domination. Second, there was the American Crisis, as the U.S. Civil War was then referred to in Europe. It was against this background of the Civil War that Marx was prompted to read about the civil wars that had beleaguered ancient Rome.

> For recreation in the evenings I have been reading Appian's "Roman Civil Wars" in the original Greek text. A very valuable book. The fellow is Egyptian by origin. Schlosser says that Appian has no "soul," probably because he is trying to discover the material bases of these civil wars "on the ground." Spartacus emerges as one of the best characters in the whole of ancient history. A great general (unlike Garibaldi), a noble character, a genuine representative of the ancient proletariat. Pompey [was] a real shit *(reiner Scheisskerl)* [who] acquired an undeserved reputation only by claiming, as Sulla's "young man," etc., Lucullus's victories [over Mithridates] and then over Sertorius [in Spain].[15]

It is not surprising that Marx compared Spartacus to Garibaldi. After all, Garibaldi's guerrillas were fighting in the same parts of Italy where Spartacus had fought his wars of liberation. Marx's admiration for Spartacus was, however, a modern sentiment. If Marx's interest in Spartacus does not seem unusual to us today, it is because the name and image of Spartacus became an important symbol of a mass political movement that shaped the course of the twentieth century—a movement provoked in part by the visions of Marx himself.

Our familiarity with Spartacus is also indebted to the way in which his image continued to be stage-managed as a political symbol in rather less romantic circumstances. Socialist movements in Europe at the end of the nineteenth and the beginning of the twentieth centuries claimed Spartacus as a symbol of resistance to economic exploitation and social inequality. But it was actually Lenin who developed the small hints in Marx's writings into a rigorous schema of a class struggle in antiquity between slaves and slave owners—defining the class struggle that characterized the Roman world as a struggle between slaves and masters[16]—ironically, a view not always shared by Marx. The way in which he did this provided the grounds for the subsequent exaltation of Spartacus in Russian and European socialist writing:

> History is full of the constant attempts of the oppressed classes to throw off oppression. The history of slavery contains records of wars of emancipation from slavery which lasted for decades.

Incidentally, the name "Spartacist" now adopted by the German communists — the only German party which is really fighting against the yoke of capitalism — was adopted by them because Spartacus was one of the most outstanding heroes of one of the very greatest slave insurrections, which took place about two thousand years ago. For several years the seemingly omnipotent Roman empire, which rested entirely on slavery, experienced the shocks and blows of a widespread uprising of slaves who armed themselves and joined together to form a vast army under the leadership of Spartacus.[17]

Most Soviet historians took their final cue for the historical significance of Spartacus from leaden hints in directives that were issued by Joseph Stalin.[18] In the official "stage theory" of history that was approved by Stalin, the Roman slave rebellions were likened to the Russian and French revolutions as armed struggles that overturned the domination of the class system of the time. Within this acceptable version of history, Spartacus suddenly assumed a new and greater importance. After all, he had actually led the final great slave war, the revolutionary armed struggle that, in Stalin's view, was the direct cause of the overthrow of the ancient slave system.[19]

This heightened importance of Spartacus as a world revolutionary figure, at the head of a transcendent stage of history, was neatly embodied in the classic work of Soviet historical writing on the subject by Aleksandr Mishulin entitled *The Spartacus Uprising*.[20] Reaping his rewards, including the editorship of the official *Journal of Ancient History*, Mishulin not unjustly credited Spartacus with his success and named his son, who later became a very popular comedian on the stage and in sitcoms on Russian television, Spartak.[21]

The Spartacus legend in the West was linked to these parallel developments in the Soviet Union. In January 1916, subversive political pamphlets began to appear in Germany bearing the signature "Spartacus" or "Spartakus." The pamphlets were protests against World War I, which was taking place at the time, and the current economic order. They were published by a left-wing political movement headed by Karl Liebknecht and Rosa Luxemburg, who named their movement the Spartakusbund (Spartacus League). Luxemburg assumed the secret name of "Junius," after Lucius Junius Brutus, who, according to legend, assassinated the last tyrant king of early Rome in 509 B.C.E. and founded the Republic. Following the assassinations of Liebknecht and Luxemburg in January 1919 and their subsequent elevation to the status of political martyrs, the figure of Spartacus became entrenched as a special historical icon in the part of Germany that later developed into the Democratic Republic of East Germany.[22] Posters and leaflets distributed in New York and Los Angeles in recent years attest to the continued existence of left-wing political groups that still identify themselves as "Spartacists."

In the late 1940s and early 1950s, people who became the victims of McCarthyism in the United States also drew on the figure of Spartacus as a paradigm of active resistance to injustice. Such ideals inspired Howard Fast, an American writer of socialist sentiments, to write the novel *Spartacus*. Mainly through the machinations and direct personal intervention of FBI director J. Edgar Hoover, Fast was blacklisted, and the book was systematically rejected by numerous publishers. He was finally forced to self-publish the novel in 1951.[23]

The Hungarian expatriate Arthur Koestler took another view of Spartacus in his novel *The Gladiators*, written in the late 1930s and reprinted in the mid-1950s, during the cold war and after the publication of Fast's *Spartacus*.[24] Koestler used the Spartacus war to sustain a perspective that was almost diametrically opposed to Fast's. He portrayed the uprising as a revolutionary movement that was inspired by high ideals but that soon degenerated into tyranny and oppression. This metaphoric vision of "the god that failed"—Koestler's condemnation of the actual practice of the ideals of European socialism under Lenin and Stalin—could not be missed.

The image of Spartacus that is arguably the most pervasive in the modern world is that of Kirk Douglas as Spartacus, mounted on a horse, sword drawn, face set in a determined, if not fierce, expression of independence. This image, grounded in the portrayal of Spartacus as a rebel underdog, was the main force that propelled the formation of the modern myth of Spartacus. In fact, after reading Fast's novel in 1957, Douglas began to identify personally with Spartacus. In his autobiography, Douglas describes his feelings as he visited various Roman ruins during his travels:

> Looking at those ruins . . . I wince. I see thousands and thousands of slaves carrying rocks, beaten, starved, crushed, dying. I identify with them. As it says in the Torah: "Slaves were we unto Egypt." I come from a race of slaves. That would have been *my* family, *me*.[25]

Although our current image of Spartacus comes primarily from these sources, if we consider the entire scope of the historical interest in Spartacus since the end of the Roman Empire, it is clear that this image was actually first created during the 1760s. Indeed, in the vast span of time before the mid-eighteenth century, no one cared about Spartacus or even mentioned him as an especially important historical character. He merited nothing more than perfunctory notices in the standard histories of Rome. It was only during the 1760s that Spartacus became "an important man."[26] The French philosopher Jean-Jacques Rousseau set the tone in some of his writings, in which he proclaimed the right of every human being to freedom and the natural right of every person to guide his or her own life. In other writings of the time, one can sense the undercurrent of romance and revolution that hailed Spartacus as a hero for the new age.[27] The historian Charles de Brosses, who was writing a history of the Roman Republic at the time, produced a detailed study of the rebellion of Spartacus, which was presented to the prestigious Academy of Inscriptions in Paris in May 1768.[28] A fellow historian, Jean Lévesque de Burigny, published a lengthy treatise on the condition of Roman slaves in 1766 and 1767, giving serious historical consideration to the Roman slave wars on Sicily and the one led by Spartacus.[29]

In 1769, Voltaire made one of the first specific references to Spartacus in the context of the justification of armed resistance to unjust oppression. In words that would later be echoed in the American Declaration of Independence, Voltaire referred to the slave war led by Spartacus as "a just war, indeed the only just war in history."[30] Perhaps more significant, however, was a popular play by Bernard Saurin titled *Spartacus: A Tragedy in Five Acts*, staged at the Théâtre Français in Paris in 1760.[31] Not only is the earlier date significant, but so is the fact that this first public presentation of Spartacus was both popular and fictional. Even at the time, the character was recognized as a fabrication, an imaginary being who responded to the current society's demands for a model of just rebellion. Saurin himself said that he wished "to evoke the picture of a great man . . . who would combine the brilliant qualities of the heroic men of justice and humanity . . . a man who was great for the good of men and not for the evil that they suffered. . . . His real aim was the abolition of slavery, whose chains he broke."[32] Saurin's play was the first artistic creation to portray the slave rebel as a symbol of the age's assertion of the individual citizen's freedoms.[33]

Rousseau, Voltaire, Saurin, and even historians such as De Burigny and De Brosses took notice of Spartacus not only because of the drive for political freedom in Europe but also because of the persistent recurrence of slave rebellions in Europe's overseas colonies. For the French, the most striking case was furnished by the island of Saint-Domingue (Haiti), where rebel slaves and freedmen led by Boukman and Toussaint L'Ouverture achieved a kind of revolutionary freedom. In the end, the plays, operas, and other theatrical representations of Spartacus were far less about the man who lived in the 70s B.C.E., or even about Roman slavery, than they were about freedom and liberty in the modern age.

Men who were not themselves slaves and had never been slaves used the image of Spartacus to think about, debate, and promote their own ideas of liberty for the citizens of the newly risen nation-states. The pattern was the same both in Europe and in the Americas. In Italy, the ideals of the independence movement led by Giuseppe Garibaldi in the mid-1800s are reflected in Raffaello Giovagnoli's huge epic novel, *Spartaco*, which was frequently reprinted and serialized after its publication in 1874.[34] The novel's "revolutionary imagery" was not accidental; it was prefaced by a glowing letter of recommendation from Garibaldi himself, written from his retreat on the island of Caprera. This novel also provided the basis for the first cinematic portrayals of Spartacus, produced in Italy during World War I.

The American play *The Gladiator* by Robert Montgomery Bird was yet another replay of the Spartacus rebellion. First produced in New York in 1831, *The Gladiator* played out the hopes and concerns of the newly confident "middle classes." Bird also was the author of plays and novels that contrasted the savage "Other"—whether Native Americans, Latin American aristocrats, or Inca princes—with the democratic ethos of the free American citizen. Bird's version of Spartacus was *the* stage success of American theater in the nineteenth century.[35] By 1854, it had been staged more than a thousand times, and it continued to play a leading role in the repertoire of the American stage for seventy years after the first production.[36]

The massive popular response to this and other such works was provoked not by any concern for the slaves themselves or for slavery as a living social institution of the time, but rather by the clarion call to liberty and freedom made to citizens who were already free. The writers who deployed these images of Spartacus were debating the legitimate status of the modern nation-state, the peculiar freedom of its citizens, and the type of liberty enshrined in its political ideals.

For all of the novelists, poets, playwrights, and filmmakers whose works appeared after the mid-1700s, the rebel slave Spartacus was a rather crude symbol for political freedom set in contrast not with real chattel slavery, least of all in nineteenth-century America, but with the fear of political tyranny, especially resurgent aristocratic forces, which might threaten democracy. In one of those odd ironies of history, Bird wrote his play the same year that Nat Turner led a slave rebellion in Virginia. Bird not only did not approve of any connection between Spartacus's drive for freedom and the rebel slaves of his own time, but he also took the opportunity to give vent to his own considerable fears:

> At this present moment there are 6[00] or 800 armed negroes marching through Southampton County, Virginia, murdering, ravishing and burning those whom the Grace of God has made their masters—70 killed, principally women and children. If they had but a Spartacus among them—to organize the half million of Virginia, the hundreds of thousands of the states, and lead them on in the Crusade of Massacre, what a blessed example might they not give to the excellence of slavery! What a field of interest to the playwriters of posterity![37]

Clearly, Bird saw the real-life slaves in American society who struck out for freedom as little more than violent criminals who were immorally protesting against a station appointed to them by God and who were therefore deserving of brute repression.

In the long, creative stream of romantic modern sentiments attached to the freedom of the individual citizen in the West's democratic states from the 1760s to the 1960s, one can count no less than half a dozen long poems, most of them heroic epics; a dozen dramas (tragedies, predictably); six operas; many paintings, intensely romantic in hue; and a score of children's books devoted to Spartacus.[38] In the twentieth century, we have seen at least six important historical novels, a ballet score by Aram Khachaturian, and several movies, mainly Hollywood-style epics.[39] By contrast, the post-1960s production of adult comic books; new wave musical forays such as Farm's 1991 "Spartacus"; and numerous jazz improvisations on the 1960 film score's theme, including Branford Marsalis's "Spartacus," also of 1991, seem only to mirror marginal discursive reflections on an icon in decadence and decline. It seems that the romantic myth of Spartacus has had its day. In a final movement of these symbols back, perhaps, to romance, the images of resistance from a position of servitude and of the bodily display of the nude male physique of the gladiator have merged to make Spartacus an icon of resistance to mainstream sexuality in the gay nightclubs of Amsterdam, in handbooks and guides to gay sex, and on similar Web pages. Everything indicates that in the first decades of the twenty-first century, the most influential images of Spartacus are changing in this new direction. For example, however much it depends on past tropes, the most recent and most popular iteration of the Spartacus story, the four-part STARZ television series, is manifestly an innovative picture that uses a new image of the rebel slave. If the element of rebellion is still in the story, the old-fashioned theme of political rebellion has been pushed into the background. The new story line, one that forefronts the sexual, cultural, and identity-based concerns of our own age, has rightly been called "'post-political' in nature."[40] In the end, we are left with the modern-day historian's questions of research and inquiry: Who was Spartacus? Who were the men and women who followed him? Why did the slave war happen when and in the way that it did? And what is its status as a historical event?

## READING GREEK AND ROMAN HISTORICAL SOURCES

Today we are so far removed from a world where servitude in manual labor was the norm that empathy alone is often our faulty guide to historical understanding. For instance, in Spartacus's day, Enna was a center of the slave economy on the island of Sicily and of the slave wars against the Roman state; now it is the home of Marina Taglialavore, the inventor of a new computer chip that has revolutionized the reading of images. Any hope of crossing this chasm to better historical understanding must begin with the fundamentals of reading the original documents that have been translated into English in this book.

In reading the sources on the three great slave wars of Sicily and southern Italy in the last generations of the Roman Republic, the student of history must first keep in mind how very rare large-scale slave wars have been in the history of the world. It is important to understand why such wars were even possible in this period and, conversely, why resistance on the level of wars did not occur in earlier or later periods of Roman history. In these other eras, sabotaging equipment, delaying the performance of work tasks, lying, stealing goods, murdering a harsh master, or simply running away were the more usual modes of resistance used by slaves. Full-scale wars were very unusual.

It is also necessary for readers to be aware of the substantial difference between the kinds of documents historians of recent times can offer their readers and those with which historians of Roman times have to cope. The collection that follows includes some original documents that have survived from the time when they were produced. Among these are laws, posters, notices, and letters concerning fugitive slaves. Just as important are minute pieces of material evidence unearthed by professional archaeologists and amateur collectors. These include the slingshot bullets that were used as ammunition by both sides in the Sicilian slave wars (Documents 42 and 55) and the coins issued under the authority of the slave leader of the first war, Eunus, under his assumed royal title "King Antiochus" (Figure 4). Although they are very small pieces of evidence, the places where they were found and the letters, markings, and the symbols with which they were decorated reveal substantive information, such as the political aspirations and religious sentiments of the rebel slaves.

Almost all of the other sources, including all of those for the Spartacus war, are taken from literary works, primarily from historians who were writing in Greek and Roman times, although some are provided by geographers, ethnographers, philosophers, and rhetoricians of the time. It is very important to remember that these documents are not in any sense reportage or simple reflections of the events in the same way that the posters on slave runaways are. Most of the documents translated in this collection were deliberately crafted, self-conscious interpretations of earlier events. It is critical to bear in mind that *not one* of these documents was written by a slave or a former slave.

It is possible to take the main sources on the Spartacus slave war as examples of the problems that plague these literary sources, but it is important to remember that the same kinds of difficulties are found in the accounts of the two slave wars in Sicily.[41] The most important written sources for any reconstruction of the Spartacus slave war are the accounts by the Roman historian Sallust, the Greek biographer Plutarch, and the Greek historian Appian. Of these three, the account by Sallust is usually deemed to be the most important, since he was closest to the events. Sallust was writing in the generation after the war. The other two writers, Plutarch and Appian, not only came from a different culture (Greek), but they also composed their accounts about two centuries after the events occurred. Each of these men necessarily depended on earlier evidence, although some modern-day historians think that both authors might have drawn on the same original source. When reading their accounts, readers must remember that these are not eyewitness reports but much later reconstructions.

All of these authors came from the affluent and privileged elites of their time. Sallust was a Roman senator. Plutarch and Appian were wealthy aristocrats with close political ties to the ruling elite of the

**Figure 2.** *The Roman Slave Trade*

This is one of the very few pictorial records that survives of a Roman slave trader. It is the gravestone of Aulus Kapreilius Timotheus, *freedman* of Aulus (that is, the slave trader was himself a former slave). He is called a *sômatemporos* or a "buyer of bodies," that is, a dealer in slaves. The stele was found near Amphipolis, a Greek city close to the shores of the northern Aegean, on the River Strymon that flowed out of regions to the north through Macedonia and Thrace (the home region of Spartacus). It was one of the major slave-trading routes connecting the eastern Mediterranean with lands to the north. The slave trader reposes on his luxurious dining couch in the top register; in the middle register are cauldrons and wine amphorae, items that were traded for the slaves who are led in a chained and manacled line in the bottom register.

Courtesy Margaret Andrews.

Roman Empire. None of these authors, whether writing history or biography, had much sympathy for slaves. Indeed, they regarded anything that was servile or tinged with the realities of slave life as inherently inferior and unworthy, and in most cases they did not even note or report it as part of their normal historical narratives. When Sallust wrote history, it was to exercise a traditional avocation appropriate to a Roman senator retired from active politics. When Plutarch composed his biographies, it was to present examples of good and bad behavior as exemplified by some of the most important and powerful men of his day. In Plutarch's view, Spartacus, a slave, was certainly *not* one of those exemplary figures. Modern readers must remember that these writers viewed the slave wars as minor elements of a more important political history. The slaves themselves were only ancillary characters in a drama where the principal actors were the wealthy and powerful men of the Greek and Roman world.

Some modern scholars have argued that it is possible to trace two different Roman historical traditions about Spartacus and that the image of Spartacus in both of them was already mythical in nature.[42] Beginning with the reports closest to the events themselves, the first tradition, reflected in the historical works of the Roman historian Livy and in the writings of the senator Cicero, is frankly hostile to Spartacus. These men, who belonged to the landowning elite of the time, viewed Spartacus and the slaves who followed him as sinister threats who deserved their fate and who were to be despised as servile people. The other tradition, as preserved in the accounts of Plutarch and Appian, seems a little more respectful of the slave leader. Spartacus is presented as a talented and dynamic commander of his forces—indeed, almost as a genuine enemy of the state. He is admired, along with other men who resisted Rome, as a brave and competent leader.[43] His death in battle is portrayed in heroic terms to evoke respect and admiration even from hostile Roman readers. These divergent pictures of Spartacus reflect the self-interest of the authors: those who, because of their property interests, tended to be dismissive of a terrible threat that would best be forgotten, as opposed to much later literary writers, who were willing to entertain the figure of a heroic and talented man who defeated a worthy enemy in a genuine war.

Many of our Roman sources have not survived the ravages of time. Plutarch's biography of the Roman senator Marcus Licinius Crassus, in which the events of the war against Spartacus are retold, does exist in its entirety. But the history written by Sallust, arguably the most original and important source on the slave war, remains only in fragments—a few pieces of manuscript and bits and pieces of the original that have survived mainly because of brief quotations by later writers. Some of these fragments are sizable, but even the longer ones have problems caused by faulty and fragmentary manuscript transmission.[44]

How, then, can we find out who Spartacus was and what he did? We must begin by recognizing the hard fact that absolutely none of his own words—and none of those of the tens of thousands of slaves who followed him into armed resistance—survive. All of those who wrote about Spartacus were, in effect, using him for their own ends. More sympathetic accounts—perhaps the treatise on the slave war written by the Sicilian rhetorician Caecilius, or the account composed by the Greek Stoic philosopher and historian Posidonius, who came from Apamea in Syria (which also was the hometown of Eunus and his wife, the leaders of the first Sicilian slave war)—probably existed. Although these accounts may have been more sympathetic, they also no doubt exploited armed rebel slaves like Spartacus as fearsome bogeymen in an attempt to show the Roman ruling elite the dangers of maltreating their subjects (now the Greeks). The covert message was, "Treat your subjects, including your slaves, humanely, and the whole system of domination of subjects by rulers will function better for all concerned."

Historians such as Posidonius, and later historians who drew on his work, such as Diodorus Siculus ("the Sicilian"), did not necessarily write more accurate accounts of the slave wars. They simply retold these stories in a way that sustained their own visions of history. For example, Diodorus (or, more probably, the source that he was using, Posidonius) tried to make a moral point by counterbalancing the evil and violent female slave owner Megallis with her kindly daughter (Documents 31 and 32). Other contemporary writers, such as Cicero, exploited Spartacus as a manifest example of a sinister insurgent who could threaten the stability of the Roman ruling order. In later generations, Spartacus would frequently be compared to the Carthaginian general Hannibal as the other "great threat" that the Romans faced.[45] Slaves and servile behavior, as much in myth as anywhere else, set notional baselines against which the Romans could measure the excellence of freeborn citizens. Nevertheless, despite the limitations of these early historians, certain basic facts—elements of time, place, person, development, scale, and pattern—have survived to give us some idea of what actually happened and why.

Taken as a whole, there exists a body of evidence from which modern historians can analyze the slave wars, not just in the history of the Roman Empire but also in the history of slavery throughout the world. But in our writing of history, whose slaves will they be? And whose version of Spartacus can we trust?

Modern artistic interpreters of Spartacus—those storytellers of liberty—have been more sympathetic to him than have professional historians. The artists feel that Spartacus deserves to be remembered—just as there was once a calculated effort to forget him, to marginalize him as insignificant in the politics and society of his time, and to discount him in the history books of our own day. They see the rebellious slave not as a premodern loser, ultimately defeated by superior Roman forces, but rather as part of a longer history of the human refusal to be subjugated.[46] Some historians have stressed the very special conditions of an unusual period in the development of slavery in Roman society that allowed these wars to happen. They also have highlighted the inability of slaves to resist successfully under most other conditions. Others feel that the Spartacus war was the kind of rebellion about which other slaves dreamed, even if they were never able to achieve their freedom by mass armed resistance. Along these lines, Howard Fast wrote,

> Tales became legends and legends became symbols, but the war of the oppressed against those who oppressed them went on. It was a flame which burned high and low but never went out. . . . It was not a question of descent by blood, but descent through common struggle.[47]

Indeed, oppressed or downtrodden people have long dreamed of a better life and a more just social order, and these dreams have a history of their own. But the two-century history of freeborn peoples using Spartacus as a provocative symbolic means of thinking about their own dreams of liberation has come to an end, and that has much to do with the use, and abuse, of Spartacus as a symbol.

## NOTES

[1]Keith R. Bradley, *Slavery and Rebellion in the Roman World, 140 B.C.E.–70 B.C.E.* (Bloomington, Ind., 1989), especially chaps. 3–5; Arnold J. Toynbee, "The Insurrections of Slaves in the Post-Hannibalic Age," chap. 9 in *Hannibal's Legacy* (Oxford, 1965),

2:313–31; and Joseph Vogt, "The Structure of Ancient Slave Wars," chap. 3 in *Ancient Slavery and the Ideal of Man* (Oxford, 1974), 39–92.

[2] Augusto Fraschetti, "Per una prosopografia dello sfruttamento: Romani e Italici in Sicilia (212–44 a.c.)," in *Società Romana e produzione schiavistica*, ed. Andrea Giardina and Aldo Schiavone (Rome, 1981), 1:51–77, traces some of the known personal connections. Also see Giacomo Manganaro, "La provincia romana," in *La Sicilia antica*, ed. Emilio Gabba and Georges Vallet (Naples, 1980), 2:411–61.

[3] Keith Hopkins, "Conquerors and Slaves: The Impact of Conquering an Empire on the Political Economy of Italy," chap. 1 in *Conquerors and Slaves* (Cambridge, 1978), 1–98; Andrea Carandini, "La villa romana e la piantagione schiavistica," in *Storia di Roma* (Turin, 1989), 101–92.

[4] See Brent D. Shaw, "A Wolf by the Ears," preface to M. I. Finley, *Ancient Slavery and Modern Ideology* (reprint; Princeton, N.J., 1998), 73f., for the main arguments and bibliography.

[5] William V. Harris, "Towards a Study of the Roman Slave Trade," *Memoirs of the American Academy in Rome* 36 (1980): 117–40; Keith R. Bradley, "Social Aspects of the Roman Slave Trade," *Münstersche Beiträge zur Antiken Handelsgeschichte* 5 (1986): 49–58; Heikki Solin, "Die Namen der orientalischen Sklaven in Rom," in *L'onomastique latine* (Paris, 1977), 205–20.

[6] Michael Crawford, "Republican *Denarii* in Romania: The Suppression of Piracy and the Slave Trade," *Journal of Roman Studies* 67 (1977): 117–24; V. Velkov, "Zur Frage der Sklaverei auf der Balkanhalbinsel während der Antike," *Etudes balkaniques* 1 (1964): 125–38; M. I. Finley, "The Slave Trade in Antiquity: The Black Sea and Danubian Regions," chap. 10 in *Economy and Society in Ancient Greece*, ed. Brent D. Shaw and Richard P. Saller (New York, 1982), 167–75.

[7] Y. Garlan, "War, Piracy, and Slavery in the Greek World," *Slavery and Abolition* 8 (1987): 7–21. For pirates and their involvement in the slave trade, see Henry A. Ormerod, *Piracy in the Ancient Mediterranean* (1924; reprint, Baltimore, 1998), especially chap. 6, which should be updated with reference to Hartel Pohl, *Die römische Politik und die Piraterie im östlichen Mittelmeer vom 3. bis zum 1. Jh. v. Chr.* (New York, 1993), esp. 161–65, 169–74, 186–90.

[8] M. I. Finley, "The Great Slave Revolts," chap. 11 in *Ancient Sicily to the Arab Conquest*, rev. ed. (London, 1979), 137–47; Peter Green, "The First Sicilian Slave War," *Past and Present* 20 (1961): 10–29; and W. G. G. Forrest and T. C. W. Stinton, "The First Sicilian Slave War," *Past and Present* 21 (1962): 87–93.

[9] Arnold J. Toynbee, "The New Plantation Agriculture in Post-Hannibalic Peninsular Italy," chap. 8 in *Hannibal's Legacy* (Oxford, 1965), 2:296–312; Martin W. Frederiksen, "I cambiamenti delle strutture agrarie nella tarda Repubblica: la Campania," in *Società Romana e produzione schiavistica*, ed. Andrea Giardina and Aldo Schiavone (Rome, 1981), 1:265–87.

[10] Arnold J. Toynbee, "The New Nomadic Animal Husbandry in Post-Hannibalic Peninsular Italy," chap. 7 in *Hannibal's Legacy* (Oxford, 1965), 2:296–312.

[11] Egon Maróti, "The *Vilicus* and the Villa System in Ancient Italy," *Oikoumene* 1 (1976): 109–24.

[12] *millenarian:* relating to mass movements powered by ecstatic personal religious experiences and a profound sense of impending revolutionary change in existing social relations.

[13] Michael Grant, *Gladiators* (1967; reprint, New York, 1995), offers some elementary facts. Much better is Thomas Wiedemann, *Emperors and Gladiators* (New York, 1992). For gladiators and their personal cult of honor, see Carlin A. Barton, "The Scandal of

the Arena," chap. 1 in *The Sorrows of the Ancient Romans: The Gladiator and the Monster* (Princeton, N.J., 1993), 1–46.

[14] "Karl Marx's 'Confession': Notebook of Jenny Marx (Zalt-Bommel, April 1, 1865)," in *Karl Marx–Frederick Engels: Collected Works* (London, 1987), 42:567–68 and plate, 569. Even for something as simple as this, there are two manuscript versions.

[15] Marx to Engels, London, February 27, 1861, *Karl Marx–Frederick Engels: Collected Works*, vol. 41 (London, 1985), 264–65. [A rather erratic English translation; the one above is my own, from K. Marx and F. Engels, *Werke* (Berlin, 1964), 30:160 (my translation).]

[16] A position subsequently repeated by Stalin and by G. E. M. de Ste. Croix, *The Class Struggle in the Ancient Greek World* (London, 1981).

[17] V. I. Lenin, "The State," in *Collected Works* 29 (Moscow, 1965), 29:481.

[18] For Stalin's views, see Mouza Raskolnikoff, *La recherche Soviétique et l'histoire économique et sociale du monde hellénistique et romain* (Strasbourg, 1975), 11–14, 127.

[19] On the role of history and the place of Spartacus in the politics of education in the Soviet Union in this period, see Raskolnikoff, *La recherche Soviétique*, 111–14 and 127–30; for Stalin's line on history, see J. Stalin, "Decisions on the Manuals of History," in *Works* (London, 1978), 14:51–55.

[20] Aleksandr V. Mishulin, *Spartakovskoe vosstanie: Revoliutsia Rabov v Rime v I do n. e.* [The Spartacus uprising: The revolution of slaves in Rome in the first century before our cra] (1936; 2nd ed., edited by S. L. Utcenko, Moscow, 1950).

[21] Wolfgang Zeev Rubinsohn, *Spartacus' Uprising and Soviet Historical Writing*, trans. John G. Griffith (Oxford, 1987), 7.

[22] Exemplified in a book by one of its leading ancient historians, Rigobert Günter, *Der Aufstand des Spartacus: Die grossen sozialen Bewegungen der Sklaven und Freien am Ende der römischen Republik* [The revolt of Spartacus: the great social movement of slaves and free men at the end of the Roman Republic] (Berlin, 1979); and by Armin Jähne, *Spartacus: Kampf der Sklaven* [Spartacus: The struggle of the slaves] (Berlin, 1986), who took the same political line.

[23] Howard Fast, *Spartacus* (1st ed., New York, 1951; reprints, New York, 1958, 1960; reprint, Armonk, N.Y., 1997).

[24] Arthur Koestler, *The Gladiators*, trans. Edith Simon (1939; 2nd ed., New York, 1956, 1962; with new postscript, New York, 1965).

[25] Kirk Douglas, *The Ragman's Son: An Autobiography* (New York, 1988), 303–4.

[26] Mouza Raskolnikoff, *Histoire romaine et critique historique dans l'Europe des Lumières: la naissance de l'hypercritique dans l'historiographie de la Rome antique* (Strasbourg, 1992), 335–41; Heinz Schulz-Falkenthal, *Sklaverei in der Griechisch-Römischen Antike: eine Bibliographie wissenschaftlicher Literatur vom ausgehenden 15. Jahrhundert biz zur Mitte des 19. Jahrhunderts* (Halle, 1985), 61–69.

[27] Wolfgang Zeev Rubinsohn, *Die grossen Sklavenaufstände der Antike: 500 Jahre Forschung* (Darmstadt, 1993), 28–30.

[28] Charles de Brosses, "La second guerre servile, ou la révolte de Spartacus en Campanie. Fragments de Salluste, tirés des IIIe et IVe livres de son Histoire générale," *Mémoires de Littérature, tirés des registres de l'Académie Royale des Inscriptions et Belles-Lettres*, 37 (1774): 23–86. De Brosses's *Histoire de la République romaine dans le course du septième siècle par Salluste* was published in 1777.

[29] Jean Lévesque de Burigny, "Premier mémoire sur les esclaves Romains . . . ," *Mémoires de Littérature, tirés des registres de l'Académie Royale des Inscriptions et*

*Belles-Lettres*, 35 (1770): 328–59; and "Second mémoire sur les esclaves romaines . . . ,"
*Mémoires de Littérature* . . . , 37 (1774): 313–39.

[30] Voltaire, *Oeuvres*, 53 = vol. 9 of *Correspondance générale*, 461–63 (Letter no. 283 of
5.4.1769).

[31] Bernard Joseph Saurin, *Spartacus, tragédie. En cinq actes, et en vers. Représentée,
pour le première fois, par les Comédiens ordinaires du Roi, le mercredi 20 février 1760*, in
*Répertoire Générale du Théâtre français* (Paris, 1818), 32:71–134. On Saurin, see Martin
Mühle, "Spartacus," in *Bernard-Joseph Saurin: Sein Leben und seine Werke* (Dresden,
1913), 44–82, who notes the direct links with Voltaire's *Brutus* (1730) in a tradition of
"anti-tyrannical" literature (p. 74f.).

[32] Rubinsohn, *Spartacus' Uprising*, 31, quoting from pp. 43 and 52 of Saurin's later
introduction to the published text of his play.

[33] Ibid., 30.

[34] Raffaello Giovagnoli, *Spartaco: racconto storico del secolo VII dell'era romana*
[Spartacus: An historical story from the seventh century of ancient Rome], illustrated by
Niccola Sanesi (Milan, 1874). Translated into many other languages; the fourth edition
(1882) featured a dramatic pictorial advertisement for *La capanna dello zio Tom* [Uncle
Tom's cabin], sold by the same publisher.

[35] Robert Montgomery Bird, *The Gladiator: A Tragedy in Five Acts*, in *The Life and
Dramatic Works of Robert Montgomery Bird*, ed. Clement E. Foust (New York, 1919),
299–440.

[36] Curtis Dahl, *Robert Montgomery Bird* (New York, 1963), 56–61. "It was said to be
the first play in the English language to be performed so often within the lifetime of the
author. . . . It was one of the greatest hits America has ever seen" (56).

[37] Richard Harris, "A Young Dramatist's Diary: *The Secret Records* of R. M. Bird,"
*Library Chronicle: University of Pennsylvania*, 25 (Winter 1959): 16–17. Bird concludes
his comments on Nat Turner's rebellion with the remark, "I had sooner live among
bedbugs than negroes."

[38] Anton J. Van Hooff, *Spartacus: De vonk van Spartacus: Het voortleven van een
antieke Rebel* (Nijmegen, 1993), offers a guide to the formation of the modern myth.

[39] Of major films, there have been three Italian versions (1913, 1914, 1953), one
American one (1960), and one Russian one (1975). See Jon Solomon, *The Ancient World
in the Cinema* (New York, 1978), 34–48; Derek Elley, *The Epic Film: Myth and History*
(Boston, 1984), 109–14; Maria Wyke, "Spartacus: Testing the Strength of the Body
Politic," chap. 3 in *Projecting the Past: Ancient Rome, Cinema, and History* (New York,
1997), 34–72; and H. I. MacAdam, "Dramatizing Roman History: Spartacus in Fiction and
Film," *Roman Archaeology Group* 10:2 (2015), 1–5.

[40] See Agoustakis & Cyrino, *STARZ Spartacus*, especially their introduction, at
pp. 1–5.

[41] Jean Christian Dumont, *Servus: Rome et l'esclavage sous la République* (Rome, 1987),
199f.

[42] Giulia Stampacchia, *La tradizione della guerra di Spartaco da Sallustio a Orosio*
(Pisa, 1976), is perhaps the best general introduction to the problems. Antonio Guarino,
*Spartaco: Analisi di un mito* (Naples, 1979), also is useful.

[43] Cicero, *Philippics*, 3.21, 4.15, 13.22; *Paradoxes of the Stoics*, 30; Fronto, *Letter to
Verus*, 2.1; Ammianus Marcellinus, *History*, 14.11.33; Scriptores Historiae Augustae
(SHA), *Life of Maximinus Thrax*, 9.6; Claudian, *Against Rufinus*, 1,255; and Sidonius
Apollinaris, *Carmina*, 3.10, are typical.

[44] *manuscript transmission:* the process of copying one manuscript from another over
a long period of time and the tendency for errors and omissions to occur in this process.

[45]Ampelius, *Liber memorialis*, 45.3; Horace, *Epodes*, 16.1–14; Horace, *Carmina*, 3.14.13–20; Porphyry, *Scholia (Notes) on Horace Carmina*, 3.14.18; Lucan, *Civil War*, 2.541–54; Pliny, *Natural Histories*, 33.49; Tacitus, *Annals*, 3.73; Eutropius, *Breviarium*, 6.7.1–2; Claudian, *On the Getic War*, 154–65; and Sidonius Apollinaris, *Carmina*, 2.235–42, 239–53, are typical of these later images.

[46]Douglas, *The Ragman's Son*, 304: "Spartacus was a real man, but if you look him up in the history books, you find only a short paragraph about him. Rome was ashamed; this man had almost destroyed them. They wanted to bury him. I was intrigued with the story of Spartacus the slave, dreaming of the death of slavery." The last part of this quote is heard at the beginning of the film *Spartacus*. Douglas anachronistically merged a dream of escape with the modern dream of abolition, but the point remains valid.

[47]Fast, *Spartacus* (1951), 363.

# PART TWO

# The Documents

# 1

# Slave Life on the Large Farms: Work, Organization, and Surveillance

On the new agricultural plantations, or latifundia, that developed in Italy and Sicily between the third and second centuries B.C.E., the core permanent labor force was made up of large numbers of slaves who had been purchased from abroad. This new type of market-oriented agriculture generated handbooks to instruct farm owners how to run a large agricultural operation. According to the ideal farm model, slaves were deployed in small work units of ten to twelve men under the close supervision of overseers. To maintain a dependable level of security over larger numbers of slaves, owners often confined them in barracks at night and when they were not working in the fields.

# 1

## COLUMELLA

## *Agricultural Slaves and the Slave Barracks*

### *First Century* C.E.

*In the following passage, the Roman agricultural writer Columella discusses the types of slaves used for heavy work in the cultivation of cereal crops. He has just finished addressing the organization and management of slaves in urban households. In offering his advice on agricultural slaves, Columella emphasizes that considerable care must be given to discipline and surveillance of the workforce.*

Columella, *On Agriculture,* 1.8.15–20.

With respect to the other slaves, these are the rules that ought to be followed. I have never had cause to regret that I have maintained them myself. As long as they have not misbehaved, I have tended to converse more often with my rural slaves in a more informal and familiar way than with my slaves in the city. When I realized that their endless regimen of work was somehow made lighter by this affability on the part of their master, I would jest with them and would even allow them to joke with me. Now I often arrange to talk with them about any new work, engaging in the pretense that they are more experienced in such matters. In this way, I become better acquainted with the abilities of each slave, and I find out just how much each slave knows. I have observed that the slaves undertake their work more willingly when they believe that they have been consulted about it and that their advice has been accepted.

It is now the usual practice for all careful masters to make certain that the slaves in the barracks are inspected, to check that they have been securely chained and that the places for housing them are secure and well guarded. The master also does this to find out whether the farm manager has chained or unchained any slave without his knowledge, since the master's orders in either case must be carefully maintained. If the head of the household has disciplined a slave by employing such a penalty, the manager of the farm must never remove the leg irons from the slave without the master's permission. Nor is the manager to release from chains any slave whom he has put in chains at his own discretion until the master has first been informed. The household head must also make an especially thorough investigation into problems involving these particular slaves. He must do so to make certain that the slaves do not suffer deprivation of clothing allotments or any other supplies that they need. Since these slaves are subject to so many persons who have authority over them, such as farm managers, work overseers, and the foremen of the slave barracks, they are more vulnerable to unjust treatment. And these slaves, once harmed by such savage cruelty or overbearing behavior, are all the more to be feared. A concerned master should therefore make inquiries both of those slaves who have been punished and of those slaves who have not been chained (whose claims are more to be trusted) to see whether they are receiving what is fair according to the master's own rules and regulations.

The master should test the bread and drink issued to the slaves by tasting it himself, and he should also inspect their clothing, gloves, and leggings. He should provide ample opportunity to the slaves to make complaints about those who have treated them cruelly or who have fraudulently cheated them. On occasion, I myself uphold the complaints of those slaves who have suffered genuine wrongs, just as I punish those who incite my slaves to rebellious behavior or who make false accusations against their overseers. On the other hand, I reward those slaves who work strenuously and assiduously at their tasks. To the more fertile female slaves, who ought to be rewarded for producing a specific number of offspring, I have allowed some respite from work. To a few of them, I have even granted freedom when they have raised an especially large number of children. When a female slave has produced three children, she is granted leave from work. When she produces more, she even receives her freedom.

Such justice and concern on the part of the head of the household contributes greatly to the increase in value of his property. But as soon as he returns from the city, he should also remember to worship the household gods. Then, if time permits (if not then, certainly by the next day), he must immediately inspect and revisit every part of his property to assess whether his absence has been the cause of any lapse in discipline and watchfulness. He must determine whether even a single vine, tree, or item of produce is missing. At the same time, he should make a careful count of the animals, slaves, and all the farm equipment and furnishings. If the master follows these procedures every year of his life, when he reaches old age he will be able to depend on a long and deeply ingrained discipline in his slaves. And he will never reach an age so old that he will be despised by his slaves.

# 2

## CATO THE ELDER

# The Vilicus: The Slave Farm Manager and His Duties

### Second Century B.C.E.

*The slave manager or bailiff, called the* vilicus *(see glossary), was one of the most important figures in the management and control of the slaves on the latifundist estates. He lived on the home farm* (villa) *and managed the labor of all the slaves who worked on the plantation—a task in which*

Cato, *On Agriculture*, 5.1–5.

*his wife, the* vilica, *also played a very important role. These managers were sometimes critical catalysts in the great slave wars, and they provided important leadership in the rebellions. The farm owners relied heavily on them to maintain slave discipline, to keep the slaves hard at work and out of trouble, and to manage the basic economic operations of the domain. The vilicus was usually required to make a thorough report to the estate owner* (dominus) *whenever the master or his agent* (procurator) *appeared to inspect the farm. The knowledge that the vilicus had of the local people, resources, and terrain was considerable and could be used, as slave owners feared, to his own advantage. The following two selections explain the duties of the vilicus and the qualifications he should have.*

These are the duties of the farm manager.

Strict order must be enforced. Religious festival days must be observed. He must keep his hands off another man's property, while diligently preserving that entrusted to him. He must settle disputes in the slave family. If a slave has done something wrong, he must be punished, but in just proportion to the wrong done. He should see that the slaves under his control do not suffer from cold or hunger. He should see that the slaves are kept hard at work, which makes it easier to keep them from getting into trouble or meddling with property belonging to others. If the manager makes it clear that he does not want the slaves to make trouble, they won't. If he allows them to make trouble, the master must not permit such behavior to go unpunished. The manager must give praise for work well done, so that the other slaves will take pleasure in behaving well. The farm manager should not be doing the rounds to ingratiate himself. Rather, he ought always to be a sober man who is not off enjoying entertainments. He should keep the slaves hard at work and see that what the master has ordered is done. He should not think that he knows better than the master. He must consider his master's friends to be his own.

The farm manager must follow the directions of whomever he has been ordered to follow. He must not perform any religious rituals without his master's permission, with the exception of the Compitalia,[1] celebrated at the crossroads, and those of the household hearth. He must not lend to anyone, and he must insist on the repayment of whatever

---

[1]*Compitalia:* a rural religious celebration that took place in late December or early January and was centered on the Roman family, including their slaves.

his master has lent. He must not make an exchange loan to anyone of seed grains, fodder, barley, wine, or oil. He should have only two or three neighboring families from whom he asks to borrow the things that he needs or to whom he lends in return, and no one else. He must review the accounts often with his master. He must not employ the same pieceworkers, wage laborers, or task workers for more than one day at a time. He must not buy anything without his master's knowledge or keep anything in secret from his master. He must not tolerate any parasitic hangers-on. He must not have any desire to consult diviners, prophets, fortune-tellers, or astrologers. He must not cheat when sowing the seed grain, since this brings bad fortune. He must make sure that he knows how to perform every agricultural task on the farm and must actually do so frequently, but never to the point of exhausting himself. If he does this, he will be able to know what is in the minds of his slaves, and they will be more willing to work for him. If he follows these practices, he will be less tempted to leave the farm, he will be healthier, and he will sleep more soundly. He must be the first to rise and the last to go to bed. Before going to bed, he must make certain that the farm is shut down correctly, that everyone is asleep in their proper place, and that the animals are provided with fodder.

# 3

## COLUMELLA

# *How to Choose a Vilicus*

## *First Century C.E.*

*Written in the first century C.E. by the agronomist Columella, the following words advise the owner of a slave-run farm on how to select the best manager or vilicus for it.*

My first warning is not to appoint a farm manager from the kind of slaves who please with their bodies and certainly not from the kind who have been engaged in effete and effeminate occupations in the city. This is a lazy and listless class of slaves who are inured to wasting time at sports

Columella, *On Agriculture,* 1.8.1–6.

fields, racetracks, theaters, gambling dens, clubs, and whorehouses, and who never stop dreaming about such frivolous things. When this type of slave brings this attitude to his agricultural work, the owner suffers loss not only in the slave himself but also to the value of his property in general. Rather, you must select a man who from childhood has been made hard by field work and who has been proven by experience. If this kind of man is not available, then choose a man from those who have shown themselves able to endure the rigors of slave labor. He should be a man who has passed beyond the first stage of youth, but who has not yet reached old age. If he's too young, his age will detract from his authority to command, since older slaves consider it beneath their dignity to obey a man who is too young. On the other hand, if he's too old, he will be broken by very hard work. He should be of middle age and of strong body and be knowledgeable in agricultural work; either that, or a man who is concerned to do a good job and who will at least be quick to learn. . . . Even an illiterate man can administer a domain rather well, as long as he has a good memory. Cornelius Celsus[1] says that this sort of domain manager more often brings money to his master than problems with his account books. Being illiterate, such a man is less able to fiddle the accounts on his own or to do it through the agency of another because of the fear that his fraud will be discovered.

Whatever type of farm manager he is, he should have a slave woman assigned to him as his wife. She will act as a restraint on him and yet will be able to assist him in performing certain tasks. The manager should be warned not to become too friendly with any slave on the farm, much less with any slave from off it. Yet he can consider it appropriate to invite a slave to dine with him on a festival day as a sort of honor or to reward a slave who has shown himself to be conscientious in the performance of his tasks and vigorous in his work regimen. He will make no sacrifices, except those made by order of the master. He must not allow prophets and witches onto the domain, since these two kinds of people incite immature and simple minds through false superstitions to make frivolous expenditures and to commit shameful deeds. He must have no knowledge of cities or the local periodic markets, except to make purchases and sales that are pertinent to the running of the farm.

---

[1]*Cornelius Celsus:* a writer during the reign of the emperor Tiberius (14–37, C.E.).

# 2

# Gladiators, Slaves, and Resistance

Gladiators were men trained to fight with a sword (*gladius*) and other weapons in order to kill or wound each other for the entertainment of spectators. Other armed professional entertainers known as beast fighters (*bestiarii*) or hunters (*venatores*) were trained to hunt wild animals such as leopards and bears for the enjoyment of large crowds. Gladiatorial games were a defining element of Roman culture as it developed in the third and second centuries B.C.E. They were first developed to their most intensive level in the region of Campania, south of Rome (Maps 3 and 4). Any analysis of the Spartacus slave war must take into account the fact that the gladiatorial schools and training facilities in this region were centered on the wealthy city of Capua. Many of our best sources of evidence about Roman gladiators, including notices for their performances, come from the city of Pompeii, located about forty-five miles south of Capua.

Gladiators often were pitted against each other to battle to the death. It is, therefore, no surprise that most of them were either condemned criminals or slaves who had little choice of their new occupation. Since gladiators were highly trained in the use of weapons and how to inflict injury on other humans, they were potentially very dangerous and had to be kept under close guard. At times, these men entered the gladiatorial arena intending to resist the fate to which they were condemned — even to the point of taking their own lives. At other times, high-ranking Romans felt that it would be advantageous to use gladiators outside the arena as professional enforcers and killers. In either case, gladiators posed a constant threat to the civil order of the Roman state in periods of political unrest and civil war.

## 4

# Graffiti on Pompeii's Walls: Gladiators and Gladiatorial Games

### First Century C.E.

*The following inscriptions were scribbled, scratched, or painted on the walls of various buildings in Pompeii, a Roman town on the Bay of Naples about forty-five miles south of Capua and immediately south of Mount Vesuvius. Most of the graffiti probably date to two or three generations after the Spartacus revolt.*

## Announcements of the Results of Individual Fights

NO. 1474

> Spiculus. From the Neronian training school. First fight. [Won.]
> Aptonetus. Freedman? 16 fights. [Killed].

NO. 2387

> Pinna. Heavy-armored Thracian gladiator from the Neronian training school. 16 fights. Won.
> Columbus. Freedman. 88 fights. Killed.

NO. 8056

> *[Graffiti above sketch of two gladiators.]*

> Severus. Freedman. 13 fights. [Killed.]
> Albanus. Freedman of Sc[aurus]. 19 fights. Won.

NO. 10237

> *[Graffiti above sketch of gladiators fighting; musicians to the right (Figure 3).]*

> Hilarus. From the Neronian training school. 14 fights. 12 crowns. Won.
> Creunus. 7 fights. 5 crowns. Discharged.
> Princeps. From the Neronian training school. 12 fights. 12 crowns.

---

*Corpus Inscriptionum Latinarum*, vol. 4. The specific number of each inscription is noted.

**Figure 3.** *Graffito from Pompeii*
The gladiators Hilarus and Creunus are engaged in hand-to-hand combat. To the right are musicians providing musical accompaniment and to the left are spectators.

*Corpus Inscriptionum Latinarum,* vol. 4, Berlin, 1898, p. 1071.

Won.
Games at Nola. To take place over four days. Marcus Cominius Heres.

# Advertisements for Forthcoming Events

NO. 1189

> The company of gladiators owned by Aulus Suettius Certus, the aedile [see glossary], will fight at Pompeii on May 31. There will also be a wild beast fight. Awnings[2] will be provided.

NO. 3882

> To the spirit of the emperor. Datius Pompeius, priest of the imperial cult, presents twenty pairs of gladiators and a wild beast hunt. The fights will take place in the town of Nuceria on May 5 and 8. Citizens of Nuceria, may you be the judges of my benefactions!

NO. 3884

> Decimus Lucretius Satrius Valens, priest for life of the emperor Nero, son of Caesar Augustus, presents twenty pairs of gladiators, and his son Decimus Lucretius Valens presents ten pairs of

---

[1]Local municipal leaders and politicians who staged gladiatorial games often announced that they would provide awnings to shade the spectators from the sun.

gladiators. They will fight at Pompeii on April 8, 9, 10, and 11. There will also be a regulation wild beast fight. Awnings will be provided.

NO. 7994

Forty-nine pairs of gladiators from the Capinian company of gladiators will fight at contests in honor of the emperors at Puteoli on May 12, 14, 16, and 18. Awnings will be provided. Magus.

NO. 9979

A wild beast hunt will be presented and twenty pairs of gladiators belonging to Marcus Tullius will fight at Pompeii on November 4 to 7.

# 5

## SALLUST

# *Gladiators as Dangerous Men: The Crisis of 63 B.C.E.*

---

*In the following passage, the Roman historian Sallust is reporting measures taken by the Senate (see glossary) upon receiving news of the outbreak of armed insurrections in various parts of Italy.*

---

In addition, the Senate decreed that if anyone would be willing to bring evidence before a court concerning the conspiracy that had been formed against the state, the reward for a slave who did so would be freedom and 100,000 sesterces [see glossary], and for a free man immunity from prosecution and 200,000 sesterces. The Senate likewise decreed that individual troupes of gladiators were to be dispersed to Capua and to the other municipalities in Italy, as the resources of each town permitted; and that night watches were to be maintained throughout the whole city of Rome and that the lower-ranking magistrates should be placed in command of them.

---

Sallust, *The Conspiracy of Catiline,* 30.6–7.

# 6

## CICERO

# *Gladiators as Dangerous Men: The Crisis of 49 B.C.E.*

*In this letter written from Cales, on the way to Capua, on January 25, 49 B.C.E., Cicero is reporting on the arrangements to quarantine gladiators owned by Julius Caesar in the crisis that followed Caesar's crossing of the Rubicon[1] and the outbreak of civil war.*

For the moment, I still hope that we can have peace, since Caesar is somewhat repentant for his mad act and Pompey [Caesar's enemy] for the lamentable condition of his forces. Pompey has expressed a wish that I go to Capua to help with the raising of troops; the farmers settled in Campania, however, are responding to the draft with little enthusiasm. The gladiators belonging to Caesar are at Capua—the ones concerning whom I was mistaken in my earlier letter to you because I was misled by false information in a letter from [Aulus] Torquatus. Pompey has quite properly dispersed these men by assigning two of them to each household head. There were 2,000 of these armed men[2] in the gladiatorial school. It was rumored that the men were just about to make a breakout. This was surely a very wise course of action to take on behalf of the state.

---

[1]In early January 49 B.C.E., Caesar led his army across the Rubicon River, which marked the boundary between his province and Italy, thereby beginning the civil war between his forces and those of Pompey the Great.

[2]Shackleton Bailey translates this as "1,000 shields" rather than 2,000 armed men.

---

Cicero, *Letters to Atticus,* 7.14.1–2 [= SB, no. 138].

## 7

JULIUS CAESAR

# Gladiators as Dangerous Men: The Crisis of 49 B.C.E.

*In his account of the first weeks of the civil war following his crossing of the Rubicon, Caesar discusses the same incident reported by Cicero in the previous selection.*

The raising of soldiers in regions around Rome was interrupted. Indeed, nothing this side of Capua [between Rome and Capua] seemed safe to anyone. They [the supporters of Pompey] first strengthened their position at Capua, collected their forces, and instituted a conscription of the farmers who had been settled on lands around Capua under the terms of the Julian Law.[1] The consul Lentulus ordered that the gladiators that Caesar had in his gladiatorial school in the city were to be brought to the forum. He encouraged their loyalty with the hope of freedom, gave horses to them, and ordered them to follow him. After he had been cautioned by his own people and his rash act had been universally condemned, Lentulus distributed the gladiators among the Roman families resident in Campania for the purpose of keeping these dangerous men under guard.

---

[1]*Julian Law:* a law passed in 59 B.C.E. under which Caesar had large numbers of veteran soldiers and poor citizens settled as agricultural colonists on public land in Campania.

Caesar, *The Civil War,* 1.14.4–5.

# 8

## TACITUS

# Gladiators as Participants in War and Rebellion

### Second Century C.E.

*The Roman historian Tacitus notes the importance of gladiators in violent insurrection. The first case is a revolt by Gallic subjects of Rome headed by Sacrovir, a tribal chieftain of the Aedui in 21 C.E., during the reign of the emperor Tiberius.*

Sacrovir [a local Gallic rebel leader] seized the town of Augusto-dunum, the tribal capital, with armed units . . . and at the same time, he distributed to the young men of the town weapons that had been manufactured in secret. By now, he had about forty thousand men under his command, one-fifth of them armed like regular legionaries, the rest of them armed with spears, knives, and other weapons used for hunting wild animals. From among the slaves, he added those men who were destined for the gladiatorial games and who, in the local style, had their entire bodies encased in armor. These men, called *cruppellarii*,[1] are not very good at inflicting blows on others but are immune to blows aimed against them.

*[Another incident recounted by the historian Tacitus occurred in 61 C.E., in the reign of the emperor Nero, in the Italian town of Praeneste, located about twenty-five miles southeast of Rome.]*

At this same time, when gladiators in the town of Praeneste attempted a breakout, they were crushed by the unit of soldiers who manned the guard over them—but not before Spartacus and other evils of the past were bandied about in gossip by the people, eager and anxious as ever for revolutionary disturbances.

---

[1]*cruppellarii:* plural of *cruppellarius,* a local type of gladiator. The precise meaning of the word is uncertain.

---

Tacitus, *Annals,* 3.43.1–2, 15.46.1.

# 9

## SENECA

# Individual Gladiators Resist Their Fate

### First Century C.E.

*In one of the letters that the Roman senator and Stoic philosopher Seneca composed to explain his philosophical views, he provided some examples of desperate resistance on the part of men who were compelled to serve as wild-beast fighters for the entertainment of Roman spectators.*

The following incident happened recently in a school that trains beast fighters. While one of the Germans was engaged in a training session for the morning spectacles, he went off to relieve himself. No other opportunity was ever allowed to him to have an unguarded moment of privacy. In the latrine, he picked up the stick tipped with a sponge which was provided for the purposes of cleaning one's obscene parts.[1] Then, jamming the whole thing down his throat, he blocked his windpipe and suffocated himself to death. What a joke to play on death! That it was, indeed. Not very genteel and not very decent. But what can be more stupid than to be overly choosy about our manner of death? What a brave man, worthy of his chosen fate. How bravely he would have used a sword. . . .

We think that the Catos, the Scipios, and others about whom we have become accustomed to listen with admiration are on a plane beyond imitation. But I will show you how even the schools for training wild-beast fighters can provide us with as many examples of courage as can generals in any civil war. Not long ago, a man was being transported (in a cart) under guard to fight in the morning spectacles. He pretended to be asleep, nodding off until he got his head low enough to shove it through the spokes on one of the wheels. He then held tightly on to his seat until the turning wheel broke his neck. He escaped his punishment by means of the very cart that was taking him to it. . . . Do you see that even the lowest of slaves, when pain provides the incitements for them, rise to the occasion and deceive even the most vigilant of guards? That is a truly great man who not only commands his own death but who also finds the death by which he is to die.

[1]Sponges were the Roman equivalent of toilet paper.

Seneca, *Moral Letters*, 70.22, 23, 25.

# 3

# Fugitive Slaves and Maroon Communities

## ROMAN LAWS ON RUNAWAY SLAVES

One of the more usual modes of resistance by slaves, and one that has parallels with the aims of larger types of collective resistance such as the slave wars, was running away. To control this behavior, slave owners used threats, the services of professional slave hunters, the force of law, and the posting of information and rewards that encouraged others to arrest and return the fugitives.

## 10

### ULPIAN

## *The Legal Definition of a Fugitive Slave*
### *Third Century C.E.*

*The following selections on runaway slaves are taken from the body of Roman laws called* The Digest, *which was compiled in the C.E. 530s by order of the emperor Justinian. The compilers of the laws collected quotations or citations from earlier Roman jurists such as Ulpian, Paul, and Callistratus—all from the early third century C.E., two centuries before Justinian's time.*

*The Digest 21.17.pr.–4, 6, 8–10. Taken from Ulpian, *The Edict of the Curule Aediles.*

Ofilius[1] defines what a fugitive slave is: A runaway is a slave who remains absent from the house of his master for the sake of flight, by which he seeks to hide himself from his master.

But Caelius says that man also is a fugitive who flees with the intent of not returning to his master but who changes his mind and returns to him. For no one, he says, who is guilty of such a grave offense becomes innocent simply because of his remorse.

Cassius writes, simply, that man is a fugitive slave who leaves his master with purposeful intent.

Likewise, in Vivianus it is stated that being a fugitive is to be determined by the man's intent . . . so that he is not a runaway who has fled from a teacher to whom he has been given for training, if perhaps he fled because he had been maltreated by the man . . . and Vivianus states the same principle if he was savagely abused by the man.

. . . Nor can that man be said to be a runaway who has come to such a state of despair that he wishes to hurl himself off a height. . . . It is simply the case that he wishes to end his own life. . . .

Caelius also writes that if you purchase a slave who then hurls himself into the Tiber River, he will not be classified as a runaway as long as he escaped from his master with the intention of killing himself. But if he planned his flight first, and then later changed his mind and threw himself into the Tiber, then he is still classified as a fugitive. He holds the same view concerning a slave who throws himself off a bridge. . . .

Likewise, Caelius states that if a slave, while he is on the farm, leaves the farmhouse with the intention of escaping but is apprehended by someone before he has got beyond the lands [boundaries] of the farm, he would seem to be a fugitive, for it is his intent that makes him a runaway.

Likewise, he states that even the slave who takes even one or two steps in flight or who just begins to run, if he is not able to evade his master who is hunting him down, is a fugitive.

For he correctly states that flight is a type of liberty, in that the slave has gained freedom from his master's power, even if only for the moment.

---

[1]*Ofilius:* This name and all the others cited in this document (e.g., Caelius, Cassius) are those of Roman jurists whose opinions are being cited.

# 11

## ULPIAN

# The Law concerning Fugitive Slaves

### Third Century C.E.

*In this selection, the third-century Roman jurist explains what laws are to apply to the constraint and punishment of runaway slaves.*

He who hides a runaway slave is himself a thief.

The Senate has decreed that fugitive slaves are not to be allowed onto rural domains, nor are they to be protected by the domain managers or by the agents of the landowners, and it has established a penalty for this crime. In the case of those persons who have either restored the runaway slaves to their owners or brought them before the municipal magistrates within twenty days, the Senate grants forgiveness for their earlier non-compliance. By the terms of the same decree of the Senate, immunity from punishment is granted to the person who, after discovering runaway slaves on his lands, returns them to their master or hands them over to the magistrates within the prescribed time.

Moreover, this same decree of the Senate has granted the right of entry to any soldier or ordinary civilian to the lands of senators or ordinary civilians for the purpose of making a search for fugitive slaves. The *Lex Fabia*[1] and a *senatus consultum* [see glossary] issued when Modestus was consul concerned this same matter. This measure [the Senate's decree] held that persons who propose to make a search for runaway slaves should present a letter to the local magistrates, and that a fine of one hundred gold pieces is to be levied against those magistrates who, when they have been presented with such a letter, fail to assist the persons making the search. Furthermore, the same penalty applies in the case of the man who does not allow such a search to be made of his property. There is also a general letter[2] issued by the emperors Marcus

[1]Lex Fabia: a law dated to the first or second century B.C.E. that legislated against kidnapping, treating a free man as a slave, or persuading another person's slave to escape.

[2]*general letter:* a decree issued by the emperor in the form of a letter to his officials that had general legal force for all the citizens of the empire.

---

*The Digest* 11.4.1–3. Taken from Ulpian, "Concerning Fugitive Slaves," in *Praetor's Edict.*

Aurelius and Commodus in which it is declared that governors, municipal magistrates, and local militia units of the army are to give assistance to owners who are searching for their runaway slaves. They are to assist with the return of the runaways who are discovered, and, further, they are to see that those persons with whom the slaves found refuge are to be punished if a crime has been committed.

Any person whosoever apprehends a runaway slave must produce him in public.

Magistrates are rightly warned that they are to guard runaway slaves carefully to keep them from escaping.

The term *fugitive* includes even the slave who "wanders off" without permission. The jurist Labeo, in his first book on the *Praetor's Edict*, however, writes that the term *fugitive* does not include a child born from a slave woman who is a runaway.

To be "produced in public" means to be handed over to municipal magistrates or to officials of the state. . . .

Fugitive slaves are to be kept under guard up to the time when they are taken before the prefect of the night watch (at Rome) or before the provincial governor.

The names of these slaves, as well as the marks on their bodies and the person to whom they belong, are to be reported to the magistrate, so that the fugitives can be more easily identified and apprehended. The word *marks* also includes scars. The law is the same if one posts the notice in writing in public or places it on a building.

Callistratus in his sixth book on judicial hearings: Simple runaways are to be returned to their owners, but if they have acted as if they were free men, they are usually punished more severely.

Ulpian in his seventh book on the duties of the proconsul [see glossary]: The emperor Antoninus Pius wrote a legal reply that if a man wishes to search for a runaway slave on another man's land, he can approach the governor of the province, who will then issue a letter to him. If the situation warrants, the governor will also assign an assistant to the man so that he will be permitted to enter the other man's property and conduct a search. The same governor shall exact a penalty from the man who does not allow his property to be searched. Likewise, the emperor Marcus Aurelius, in a speech that he read in the senate, granted the right of entry to imperial as well as senatorial and private lands to those who wish to search for fugitive slaves, and he permitted them to make a thorough search for the tracks and the hiding places of those who are concealing runaways.

## FUGITIVE SLAVE POSTERS

The following letters and public posters about runaway slaves are some of the most striking of the original documents on slavery that have survived from Roman times. This is because they were written on papyrus, an early form of paper, and by good fortune they were preserved by the hyperarid environment in the Roman province of Egypt. This province was divided into districts, or *norms*, each of which was headed by a local administrator called a *stratêgos*, who resided in the capital city or metropolis of the nome. By studying these documents as a group, we can speculate about the conditions under which slaves tried to escape the conditions of their lives, which ones tended to run away (individuals or groups, men or women), and where they went.

**12**

*A Census Declaration Including Notices*
*on Runaway Slaves, Tebtunis, Egypt*

*189 C.E.*

---

*The first part of the document, which is a typical tax declaration of property, has been omitted here. We begin with the fourteenth line, where the woman—Isidôra, daughter of Paeos—who is filing the tax statement declares the persons (property) whom she owns.*

---

. . . which (property) I am registering in the house-by-house census of the aforementioned village for the 28th year, just completed, of Our Lord Emperor Aurelius Commodus Antoninus Caesar. I (the declarant), named Isidôra, 60[+] years of age, and my slaves [literally, "slave bodies"]: Philoumenê, 45 years old, and her offspring Dioskouros, 8 years old, and Athenarios, 4 years old; and another slave, Elephantinê, offspring of Dêmêtria, 20 years old, and her offspring Eudaimonis, 5 years old, and Isaurous, 1 year old; and another female slave, Helenê, who has run away, 68 years old; and Ammônarion, 42 years old, and Herakleia, 38 years old, who have also run away. I thus declare in year 29 of Our Lord Emperor Aurelius Commodus Antoninus Caesar, Mesore 19 [about mid-August].

---

P. Berlin Leihg., 15.

# 13

## A Declaration Concerning a Runaway Slave, Egypt

### August 13, 156 B.C.E.

*The following papyrus document from Roman Egypt is a public announcement posted by a slave owner seeking the capture and return of one of his runaway slaves.*

YEAR 25; EPEIPH 16 (ABOUT MID-JULY)
A slave [literally, "a boy"] belonging to Aristogenes, son of Chrysippos, ambassador from Alabanda, has run off to Alexandria.

Name, Hermôn, also known as Neilos; Syrian by birth, from the city of Bambykê, age about eighteen; medium height, no beard, well formed legs, cleft in his chin, mark near the left side of his nose, scar above the left corner of his mouth, right wrist tattooed with "barbarian" [non-Greek] letters.

Took with him when he fled: a belt containing three gold coins weighing three minae [see glossary] and ten pearls; an iron ring on which were an oil flask and some body scrapers; clothing on his body—a short riding cloak and a loincloth.

The one who returns him will receive two (later raised to three) talents [see glossary] of bronze; the one who hands him over to a temple authority will receive one talent (later raised to two talents); if it is to a man of good standing and one who can be sued, the reward will be three talents (later raised to five).

If anyone wishes to file information [on the above notice], he should do so to the assistants of the stratêgos.

Also ran away with him: one Biôn, a slave belonging to Kallikrates, one of the chief servants of the court—small in stature, wide-shouldered with thinnish legs, bright-eyed. He had with him when he fled: a tunic, a small slave's cloak, a woman's jewelry box worth six talents, and five thousand bronze pieces.

The one who returns him will receive the same rewards as in the first case noted above. Make the same type of declaration, as above, to the assistants of the stratêgos.

P. Paris, 10.

# 14

## Posters for Runaway Slaves, Oxyrhynchus, Egypt
### Third Century C.E. (?)

---

*These are notices posted by individual owners who are looking for runaway slaves and so specify the ways by which they can be identified.*

---

If any person finds a slave named Philippos . . . about fourteen years old, light in complexion, who speaks haltingly, has a flat nose . . . wearing a . . . woolen garment and a used shoulder belt, he should bring him to the army post and receive . . .

[A slave by the name of Ho]ros(?), an Egyptian, from the [village of] Chenrês in the nome of Athribis [in the Delta], who does not know how to speak Greek, a tall man, thinnish, clean shaven, who has a scar on the left side of his head, somewhat tan in complexion, rather pale, with almost no beard, in fact not having any hair where his beard should be, smooth, narrow in the chin, long-nosed. A weaver by occupation, he struts around arrogantly, speaking in a harsh voice. Age about thirty-two. He is wearing naturally dyed clothes. He has . . .

---

P. Oxy., 3616, 3617.

# 15

## A Legal Notice Concerning a Runaway Slave, Oxyrhynchus, Egypt
### ca. 250–270 C.E.

---

*This is a petition from a female slave owner to the Roman administrator of the local district (*nome*) concerning one of her escaped slaves and his thefts.*

---

To Aurelius Prôtarchos, also named Herôn, stratêgos of the nome of Oxyrhynchus, from Aurelia Sarapias, also named Dionysarion, daughter

---

of Apollophanes, also named Sarapammon, exegete[1] of the city of Antinöopolis, who does not require a legal guardian because of the right of [three] children that she has acquired.

I have a slave named Sarapion, who formerly belonged to my father. I believed that he had done nothing wrong while he was part of my father's property, and so he was entrusted by me with our possessions. This man—I do not know just how—in connivance with other low persons, managed to despise the position of respect and the provisions for his upkeep that we had given him and stealthily removed several things from our household, including cloaks and other possessions, which he took with him when he fled and which he then sold, and . . . he now resides in the settlement of Chairêmon in the nome of. . . . I request that . . . to the peace officer Aurelius in the nome of . . . *[the manuscript is defective.]*

# 16

# *Authorization for the Arrest of a Fugitive Slave, Oxyrhynchus, Egypt*

## *Fourth Century C.E.*

*One Roman official writes to another official giving him the right to find and arrest one of his runaway slaves.*

Flavius Ammônas, official on the staff of the governor of the province of Egypt, to Flavius Dôrotheos, official: Greetings.

I order you and deputize you to arrest my slave, named Magnus, who is a runaway and is now to be found in the town of Hermopolis. He stole certain possessions of mine. Bring him bound in chains to the man in charge of Sesphtha [a subdistrict of the nome of Oxyrhynchus]. This order has full government authority. When requested, [you should state that] I gave my assent: I, Flavius Ammônas, official on the staff of the governor of the province of Egypt, have issued this order.

---

[1]*exegete:* a town official or magistrate in Roman Egypt who combined the functions of a census official and an aedile.

---

P. Oxy., 1423.

# A Roman Praetor in Sicily Hunts Down Runaway Slaves

## 131–130 B.C.E.

*The following document is a text inscribed on a stone plaque found at Polla, in southern Italy. It records the achievements of an unknown Roman magistrate who was praetor in the Roman province of Sicily and was engaged in the rounding up of fugitive slaves there, probably in the immediate aftermath of the first slave war. Subsequently, he constructed a major road beginning at Capua, which was later the center of the outbreak of the Spartacus slave war, perhaps to facilitate troop and supply movements from central Italy to Sicily, should another slave insurrection occur. The events in the inscription probably refer to the years 131–130 B.C.E. and those immediately following.*

I constructed the road from Rhegium to Capua, and I built all of the bridges for this road and placed all of the milestones and signs on it. From here [to the north] it is 51 miles to Nuceria, 84 miles to Capua; [to the south], 74 miles to Muranum, 123 miles to Consentia [Cosenza], 180 miles to Valentia, 231 miles to Statua [the statue?] on the Strait of Messana [Roman spelling of Messina], and 237 miles to Rhegium. The total number of miles from Capua to Rhegium is 321. Also, when I was praetor in Sicily, I hunted down runaway slaves that belonged to Italians and returned 917 men to their owners. Also, I was the first man to make shepherds yield ground to farmers on the public lands that belong to the Roman people. At this place, I constructed a forum and its public buildings.

## MAROON COMMUNITIES

Sometimes runaway slaves coalesced in sufficient numbers in locations far enough from the control of the state and its regulatory forces that they were able to establish permanent autonomous communities. These communities, often located in the mountain highlands of

*Corpus Inscriptionum Latinarum,* vol. 1, no. 638 = vol. 10, no. 6950 = *Inscriptiones Latinae Liberae Rei Publicae,* no. 454 (vol. 1, 253–55) = *Inscriptiones Italiae,* vol. 3, fascicle. 1, no. 272.

the Mediterranean, were reasonably free from the interference of state authorities and the private enforcers of slave owners. Historians usually call them maroon communities, based on similar communities established during the sixteenth to nineteenth centuries in the Caribbean and the Americas, where this behavior was known as *marronnage*. Aside from fictional accounts, there are not many detailed reports of maroon communities in ancient historical sources. The selection from Cicero dates from a few decades after the Spartacus war. The account of the escaped slave Drimakos gives us a brief glimpse into one hope of escape that slaves might have had before the Roman slave wars. The selection from Cassius Dio on the bandit Bulla Felix is from a later period in Roman history.

# 18

## CICERO

## *Free Communities in Cilicia Harbor Runaway Slaves*

### *51–50 B.C.E.*

*In the following letter, the Roman senator Cicero is reporting on his year (51–50 B.C.E.) as governor of the Roman province of Cilicia, in what is today the far southeastern corner of Turkey and the northernmost parts of Syria and Lebanon. As governor of Cilicia, Cicero had to battle free highland peoples in the Taurus and Amanus mountain ranges whose communities were a natural refuge for runaway slaves.*

When I had completed this business, I led the army to Pindenissum, a village of the free Cilicians. The town is located on a very high and well-defended site, and it is inhabited by people who have never given obedience, even to kings, which is shown by the fact that they regularly receive runaway slaves. . . . I thought that it was important for the prestige of our rule that their arrogance and audacity be crushed—then it would be easier to break the spirits of the other peoples in the region who are hostile to our authority.

Cicero, *Letters to His Acquaintances,* 15.4.10.

## ATHENAEUS

# Drimakos: The Fugitive Slave Bandit King

### Second Century C.E.

*The second-century writer Athenaeus, in his enormous compendium of the conversations of philosophers at a banquet, relates the story of the bandit king Drimakos, who may have lived in the late fourth or early third century B.C.E. It is one of the more detailed tales that we have concerning the founding of a maroon community. In reading this story, note the peculiar topography, which permitted the existence of an independent community even on a small island like Chios. Also important are the negotiated relationships that developed between Drimakos, the head of the maroon community, and the community of free Greek citizens on the island.*

The people of the island of Chios were the first Greeks, that I know, who used slaves that they had purchased with money, as Theopompos tells us in the seventeenth book of his *Histories*:

> After the Thessalians and the Spartans, the people of Chios were the first Greeks to use slaves; but the Chians did not acquire their slaves in the same way as did the former peoples. For, as we shall later see, the Thessalians and the Spartans created their slave force out of Greeks, who were the earlier inhabitants of the same lands that they now control. The Spartans took over the territory of the Achaians; the Thessalians . . . [took over the lands] of the Perrhibaioi and the Magnesians. The Spartans call their indigenous enslaved peoples Helots, whereas the Thessalians call theirs Penestai. But the Chians acquired people who were not Greek speakers to be their slaves by paying a price for them.

This is what Theopompos tells us. In my view, the divinity punished the people of Chios for this deed, since in later times they were engaged in a long war because of their slaves.

Nymphodoros of Syracuse tells the following story in his book *Voyage along the Coast of Asia Minor.*

---

Athenaeus, *Deipnosophistae*, 6.265d–66d.

The slaves of the Chians ran away and sought refuge up in the mountains. They gathered there in large numbers and then proceeded to do great damage to the rural holdings of the Chians. The island of Chios is rugged and covered with forests. There is a story that the Chians tell. A little before our own time, a certain slave ran off to make his home up in the mountains. Since he was a brave man who had a lot of luck when it came to fighting, he became the leader of the fugitive slaves in the same way that a king is the commander of an army. The Chians made many armed forays against him, but with no success. Drimakos, for this was the fugitive slave's name, realized that everyone was being killed and for no good reason. So he made the following proposal to the people of Chios:

> Slave owners of Chios!
> The damage that you have been suffering because of your slaves is never going to cease. How can it, since such things are happening in accordance with an oracle of the god? But if you make an agreement with me, we can all live in peace, and I will guarantee many benefits for you.

The people of Chios decided to make a treaty with Drimakos and so agreed to a truce for a limited period of time. For his part, Drimakos had some weights and measures and a special seal made. He showed these to the Chians and announced to them:

> Anything that I seize from you will be taken in accordance with these weights and measures. When I have taken whatever it is that I need, I will leave your storerooms closed with this seal of mine. Furthermore, I will interrogate any of your slaves that run away about the reasons for their flight. If any one of them seems to me to have run away because he or she has been maltreated in any way, I will keep that person with me. But if I don't find their story to be persuasive, I will send them back to their owners.

When the other slaves saw that the people of Chios were ready to make this agreement, they ran away much less often. They were afraid of being interrogated by Drimakos. By the same token, the fugitive slaves who were living with Drimakos feared him much more than their own masters, and so treated him with great respect and obeyed him as if he were their commander. Drimakos punished those who were guilty of breaches of discipline and did not allow anyone to plunder the fields or to commit even a single illegal act without first having obtained his permission to do so. During the period of the religious festivals on the island, he would confiscate wine and animals from the fields that were proportionate to the required sacrifices—but only if the owners themselves did not hand them over first. If he discovered anyone who was planning to set an ambush against him, he would take immediate vengeance on him.

Finally, the city-state of Chios announced that it would give a large sum of money to any person who captured Drimakos alive or who brought in his head. So, at the end of his life, when he had grown old, Drimakos summoned his boyfriend to a specific place and told him: "I have loved you more than anyone else. You have been my favorite and like a son to me," and so on and so forth . . . and then continued:

> I have lived long enough now, while you are still a young man with the best years of your life before you. So what should be done? You should become an honest and respected citizen. Since the government of Chios has promised to give a large sum of money to the man who kills me and has also promised to grant that man his freedom, it is you who must cut off my head and take it to the Chians. Then you must claim the money from the state and live out your life as a fortunate man.

Although the young man protested, Drimakos persuaded him. So he cut off Drimakos's head and collected the reward money that the Chians had promised. He then buried the body of the old fugitive slave and left Chios to settle back in his homeland.

Afterward, however, the people of Chios suffered greatly from attacks on their property and from thefts made by their slaves, just as they had in the days before Drimakos. Only then did they remember how fair and just Drimakos had been with them when he was alive. So they constructed a shrine to him out in the countryside and dedicated it to "Our Benevolent Hero." Even in our own day, runaway slaves bring the first fruits of everything that they steal to consecrate to him. It is also reported that Drimakos appears to many Chians in their dreams when they are asleep and warns them when their slaves are plotting against them. These persons, to whom he has manifested himself in visions, go to the place where the hero's shrine stands and make sacrifices to him.

This is the account given by Nymphodoros. But in many of the manuscripts, I have found that the texts do not actually specify Drimakos by name.

# 20

## CASSIUS DIO

# Bulla Felix: The Bandit King

### Third Century C.E.

*The following story, taken from the history of Cassius Dio, tells of an incident of brigandage in Italy in the reign of the Roman emperor Septimius Severus (193–211 C.E.). The tale illustrates the close linkages between banditry, fugitive slaves, and the formation of maroon communities.*

At this time [in the years after 205 C.E.], an Italian man named Bulla collected a bandit gang of about six hundred men and staged bandit raids throughout Italy for a period of two years, despite the presence of the emperors and a large number of their soldiers. Although many men pursued Bulla, and the emperor Severus himself tracked the man zealously, he was never seen when seen, never found when found, never caught when caught. In part this was because of Bulla's great generosity with gifts and his intelligence. For Bulla got to know everything about the people who departed from the city of Rome, as well as all of those who disembarked at the port of Brundisium. He knew who they were, how many of them there were, what sorts of possessions they had with them, and how much they had. From some of these persons, he would take a portion of their goods and then would immediately send them on their way. Those among them who were craftsmen, however, he would detain for a time, make use of their skills, and then send them on their way with a gift.

When two of his bandits were captured and were about to be thrown to the wild beasts as punishment, Bulla went to the prison guard, pretending that he was the official in charge of that part of the country, and asked to have two particular men of the type that he needed handed over to him. He managed to save their lives by requisitioning them in this way. Indeed, Bulla actually approached the centurion who had been sent out to destroy his bandit gang. Bulla did this first by laying charges against himself while pretending to be someone else; he then promised the centurion that if he followed him, he would betray the bandit chief to the officer. In this way, Bulla led the centurion into a narrow

Cassius Dio, *Histories,* 76/77.10.1–7.

defile,[1] a heavily forested place, as if he were leading him to Felix (for the bandit chief was also known by this name), and so easily captured the centurion. Some time later, donning the official dress of a Roman magistrate, Bulla mounted a tribunal[2] and ordered the centurion, whose head he had had shaved, to be arraigned before him. He said, "Tell your slave masters that they should feed their slaves enough so that they do not turn to a life of banditry." For most of the men whom Bulla had recruited were slaves from the emperor's household, some of whom had received little remuneration[3] and others who had received no sustenance whatsoever.

When the emperor Severus learned of these events, he was terribly angry. At the very time that he was defeating foreign enemies in Britain through his legates [see glossary], he himself was being defeated in Italy by a mere bandit. Finally, he dispatched a tribune[4] of his own bodyguards with a large detachment of cavalry. He threatened the man with terrible punishments if he did not bring Bulla back alive. When this man learned that Bulla was having an affair with another man's wife, by using a promise of immunity he persuaded the woman, through her husband, to assist him. The result was that the bandit was arrested while he was asleep in one of his caves.

When Bulla was put on trial, Papinian, the praetorian prefect [see glossary], asked him, "Why did you become a bandit?"

Bulla retorted, "Why did you become praetorian prefect?"

Later, after a formal proclamation of his guilt was made, Bulla was thrown to the wild beasts. His gang of brigands disintegrated, so much did the whole strength of his six hundred men depend on him alone.

---

[1]*defile:* a narrow passage or gorge.
[2]*tribunal:* the official platform of a Roman magistrate.
[3]*remuneration:* recompense.
[4]*tribune:* high-ranking military officer.

# 4

# Slave Revolts in Italy and Sicily Before the Great Slave Wars

In the second major war that Rome fought with Carthage (218–201 B.C.E.), the Carthaginian commander Hannibal ravaged Italy south of Rome, while Roman forces devastated the parts of Sicily controlled by the Carthaginians and their allies. After the war, general conditions of peace and prosperity returned to southern Italy and Sicily. The half-century after 200 B.C.E., however, witnessed several slave rebellions. For information on most of these outbreaks, we are dependent on the year-by-year (annalistic) account of the Roman historian Livy. He reports continuing, though small-scale, episodes of violent slave resistance in southern Italy, which the Roman authorities categorized as "conspiracies." These uprisings seem to have been linked with the cult of the god Bacchus, also known as Dionysus.

## 21

## LIVY

## *Slave Rebellions at Setia and Praeneste in 198 B.C.E.*

### First Century B.C.E.

*The historian Livy, writing at the end of the first century B.C.E., records minor slave revolts in two towns in Italy close to Rome.*

Livy, *History of Rome*, 32.26.4–18.

Although Gaul was more peaceful than expected that year, slave insurrections broke out in regions close to the city of Rome. The hostages that the Carthaginians had handed over were being kept under guard at Setia, and since they were the sons of the leading men at Carthage, a great number of slaves had accompanied them. Because of the recent war in Africa, the numbers of these slaves had further increased, since the people of Setia themselves had purchased slaves from the African prisoners of war who had been seized as war booty. When these slaves formed a conspiracy, they first dispatched members of their group to ask the slaves in the rural lands around Setia to join them. Later they approached the slaves around Norba and Cerceii. When all their preparations were ready, the slaves decided to attack the people who would be coming to watch the spectacles that were to be staged at Setia while their attention was focused on the games. By murder and the suddenness of their uprising, the slaves were able to take over Setia, but they were not able to capture Norba or Cerceii.

Witness of this dreadful event was brought to Rome and reported to the urban praetor, Lucius Cornelius Lentulus. Two slaves came to him before dawn and told the story, step-by-step, of all that had happened and also revealed to him what future actions were being planned. The praetor ordered these men to be kept under guard at his house and then summoned the Senate to inform it of what he had been told. Lentulus received orders from the senate to make an investigation into the conspiracy and to suppress it. He departed from the city with five legates. To any men that he encountered on his way, he administered the soldier's oath and compelled them to take up arms and to follow him. With this emergency force of nearly two thousand armed men, Lentulus arrived at Setia before anyone was aware of his movement. After his quick arrest of the leaders of the conspiracy, there was a general flight of the slaves from the town. His troops were then sent throughout the fields around the town to hunt down the fugitives.

Because of the outstanding public service of the two slaves and the one free man who had provided evidence on the conspiracy, the senate ordered that the free man be given a reward of 100,000 asses [see glossary], and that each of the slaves was to be given a reward of 25,000 asses together with a grant of freedom. The value of the slaves to their former owners was reimbursed to their masters by the state treasury.

Not much later, it was reported that remnant elements of the same slave conspiracy were planning to seize the town of Praeneste. Setting out from Rome, the praetor Lucius Cornelius executed approximately five hundred men who were guilty in this affair. In the city of Rome, there was fear that the Carthaginian hostages and prisoners of war were involved. Therefore, even at Rome, night watches were maintained throughout the neighborhoods of the city, and the lower-ranking magistrates were ordered to patrol them, while the triumvirs[1] in charge of the underground prison were ordered to maintain a more vigilant guard over it. Moreover, a letter was sent around by the praetor to the member cities of the Latin Name [see glossary] to the effect that the hostages were to be kept under guard in private homes and that they were not to be given any freedom to go out into public places. The letter also cautioned that the prisoners of war should be bound with leg irons of not less than ten pounds weight, exactly as if they were being confined in a state prison.

## 22

### LIVY

## A Slave Rebellion in Etruria Is Suppressed in 196 B.C.E.

### First Century B.C.E.

*The historian Livy, writing at the end of the first century B.C.E., records an outbreak of slave resistance in the region of Etruria (modern Tuscany) just to the north of Rome in central Italy.*

When these events were taking place in Greece, Macedonia, and Asia, a slave conspiracy created a great danger in Etruria. Manius Acilius Glabrio, the praetor who exercised jurisdiction between citizens and foreigners, was dispatched with one of the two legions [see glossary] in the city to investigate and to repress the rebellion. Some of the slaves he . . . *[manuscript is defective],* while he defeated in battle others who had already congregated in groups. Many of these were killed, and many others were taken prisoner. Some of the slaves, who were the leaders

---

[1]*triumvirs:* a board of three state officials or magistrates.

---

of the conspiracy, Glabrio ordered to be crucified after they had been whipped. Others he returned to their masters.

**23**

**LIVY**

## Actions of Roman Praetors in Bruttium and Apulia in 190 B.C.E.

### First Century B.C.E.

---

*In the next three items, military actions taken by praetors in southern Italy are recorded. Although the precise reason for their armed presence in Apulia and Bruttium is not specified, given the record of operations conducted by praetors in these regions in 186–182 B.C.E. (Documents 28–30), there is every reason to believe that the repression of Bacchanalian conspiracies and slave shepherds also took place in these earlier years.*

---

The praetors then drew lots for the assignment of their provinces. . . . The two urban legions, which had been conscripted in the previous year, together with fifteen thousand infantry and six hundred cavalry from the allies and the communities of the Latin Name, were assigned to the praetor Marcus Tuccius to enable him to govern Apulia and the Bruttii. Aulus Cornelius, who had been praetor in the previous year, had governed the Bruttii with an army . . .

---

# 24

## LIVY

## Roman Praetors in Bruttium and Apulia in 189 B.C.E.

### First Century B.C.E.

*The historian Livy, writing at the end of the first century B.C.E., records military operations by Roman army commanders, praetors, in southern Italy.*

As for the magistrates from the previous year, a prorogation [see glossary] of command for one year with an army was ordered . . . [including the command] of Marcus Tuccius, propraetor [see glossary] over the Bruttii and Apulia.

Livy, *History of Rome,* 37.50.13.

# 25

## LIVY

## Roman Praetors in Bruttium and Apulia in 188 B.C.E.

### First Century B.C.E.

*The historian Livy once again (Documents 23–24) records military operations by Roman army commanders, praetors, in southern Italy.*

Concerning the armies, the following was decided: that the legions which were under the command of Gaius Laelius were to be removed from Gaul and transferred to Marcus Tuccius, the propraetor over the Bruttii.

Livy, *History of Rome,* 38.36.1.

# 26

## LIVY

# The Bacchanalian Conspiracy at Rome in 186 B.C.E.

## First Century B.C.E.

*In 186 B.C.E., a "great fear" swept through the Roman state, an apprehension that was somehow connected with perceptions of social subversion and a panic related to the supposed seepage of strange and insidious foreign cults into Roman society. These fears were centered on the worship of the god Bacchus, or Dionysus, whose worship, it was felt, transgressed the rather rigid Roman social barriers between men and women and between free persons and slaves.*

Both consuls of the year were ordered to make a judicial investigation into hidden conspiracies. A certain low-class Greek man had come to Etruria first. He did not have any of those skills which that most learned of all peoples bring for the education of our minds and bodies. He was just a small-time sacrificer and prophet. He was not the kind of man who made open and public profession of his religious practice and one who, by openly preaching his ideals and his system, filled people's minds with wrong ideas. Far from it. He was instead the priestly leader of secret nocturnal rites. At first, the initiation rituals were made known only to a few, but they were later opened up to the common run of persons, both men and women. To the religious rituals themselves were added the sensual pleasures of wine and food so that the minds of many more people would be attracted to the cult. When wine had inflamed their desire, and it was night, and the mixing of males with females and of persons of tender youth with older persons extinguished all vestiges of shame, every kind of lewd behavior began to be practiced. After all, everybody had right at hand the sort of sex to which they were driven by the sexual impulses peculiar to them. The illegal sexual liaisons of free men and free women were not the only type of crimes that were being committed. Perjured witnesses, forged signatures on wills and testaments, and false evidence all emerged from this same workshop. Poisonings and the murders of relatives were arranged in such a way

Livy, *History of Rome*, 39.8.3–9.1, 17.4–6, 18.7.

that not even the bodies could be found for proper burial. Many of these crimes were accomplished by stealth, but more were brazenly done by the use of brute force. Human howling and the clashing of drums and cymbals concealed these acts of violence. Nobody who cried out could be heard amid the sexual orgies and the slaughter. The lethal poisons of this evil spread from Etruria to Rome like a contagious disease. At first, the size of the city, which was large and capable of enduring these evils, enabled them to remain hidden. But, finally, evidence of them came to the consul [Spurius] Postumius in the following way.

*[An elaborate story follows that involves a young Roman male citizen named Aebutius and an ex–slave woman named Hispala Faecenia. It is through this freedwoman that the consul and then the Senate at Rome learned details of the Bacchanalia, or the rituals associated with the worship of Bacchus, by "cult cells" in the city. These discoveries were shocking and provoked a general panic among the citizenry and widespread retaliatory actions by the Senate.]*

When the public assembly was dismissed, a great fear seized the entire city, and not only the core parts of the city itself or its territory but the whole of Italy. When letters concerning the decree of the Senate, the public meeting, and the edict of the consuls were received by local men in Italy who were well connected with high-ranking men at Rome, panic began to spread. That same night, people trying to flee the city were arrested and brought back to Rome, and the names of many other people were given to the authorities by informers. Some of these people, both men and women, took their own lives. It was said that more than seven thousand men and women were involved in the conspiracy. . . . The task of eradicating all Bacchanalian practices, first at Rome, then throughout all of Italy, was assigned to the consuls. *[For this decree of the Senate, see document 27 following.]*

# 27

# *Measures Decreed by the Roman Senate concerning the Bacchanals*

## *186 B.C.E.*

*The Bacchanalia were characterized by millenarian expectations that encouraged the adherents to transgress the conventions of the established*

*Corpus Inscriptionum Latinarum,* I², no. 581 = vol. 10, no. 104 = *Inscriptiones Latinae Liberae Rei Publicae,* no. 511 (vol. 2, 13–17).

*social and political order. Ecstatic or highly emotional out-of-body expe-*
*riences transformed the identity of the believer. Bacchic rituals blurred*
*not only gender boundaries between men and women but also status*
*boundaries between slave and free. The Bacchanalia were therefore*
*consistently associated with slave resistance in southern Italy. The consuls*
*of 186 B.C.E. held wide-ranging investigations and trials throughout Italy*
*to enforce the decree of the Senate. Fortunately, we have a copy of the*
*orders issued by the Senate to the consuls by which the cult was to be con-*
*trolled. It survives on a bronze plaque from Tiriolo in Bruttium, the "toe"*
*region of southern Italy. Taken together with the concerns about the links*
*between slave "conspiracies" and Bacchic groups in southern Italy before*
*and after 186 B.C.E., this evidence reveals a powerful connection between*
*religious sentiment, cult organization, and attempts by the state to control*
*the dangerous aspects of this behavior.*

Quintus Marcius, son of Lucius, and Spurius Postumius, son of
Lucius, the consuls, advised the Senate on the 7th of October in the
Temple of Bellona. Present at the drafting were Marcus Claudius, son
of Marcus; Lucius Valerius, son of Publius; and Quintus Minucius,
son of Gaius. They moved that the following measure concerning the
Bacchanals ought to be decreed to those communities allied to Rome
by treaty:
— Let none of them wish to have a Bacchic cult group. If by chance
 there is any one of them who believes that they must have such a
 cult group, they must come before the urban praetor at Rome so
 that their arguments might be heard and our Senate might issue
 a decree on the matter—as long as no fewer than one hundred
 senators are present when the matter is debated.
— Let no Roman citizen or person of the Latin Name [see glossary]
 or ally of the Roman people whosoever wish to be present with
 Bacchic women unless they have first approached the urban
 praetor and he grants his approval pursuant to a decree of the
 Senate—as long as no fewer than one hundred senators are
 present when the matter is debated.
So decreed.

— Let no man be a priest. Let no man or woman whosoever be a
 chief officer of the cult. Likewise, let no one wish to maintain a
 common treasury. Similarly, let no man or woman whosoever
 wish to be made an officer or to act in the place of an official of

the cult. Nor shall they wish, from this point forward, to swear an oath among themselves or to make a common vow or to form any pacts or make promises in common, nor should anyone whosoever give pledges among themselves. Nor should anyone whosoever wish to perform sacred rituals in secret. Nor should anyone whosoever wish to perform any sacred rituals, whether in public or in private or outside the city, unless he shall first have approached the urban praetor and he grants his permission pursuant to a decree of the Senate—as long as no fewer than one hundred senators are present when the matter is debated.

So decreed.

— Let no person whoever wish to perform sacred rituals with more than five men or women, and let there be present in a group at that place no more than two men and no more than three women, unless by permission of the urban praetor pursuant to a decree of the Senate, as written above.

*[The text above is from the decree of the Senate; what now follows are the orders of the consuls to the local community in the Ager Teuranus[1]]*

— You shall announce these measures to a public gathering at no less than three market days, and so that you might know the decision of the Senate, that this is its decree: If there is anyone who acts contrary to this measure, as it is written above, they have decreed that a capital charge shall be laid against them.

— That it is rightful that you shall cause this measure to be incised on a bronze tablet and that you shall order it to be fastened to a place where its contents can easily be known; and that you shall see to it that those Bacchanalian groups that still exist, and which are outside those deemed sacred and acceptable as described above, shall be dispersed within ten days after these tablets will have been delivered to you.

In the Ager Teuranus.

---

[1]*Ager Teuranus:* the rural area in the region of Bruttium (Map 4).

## 28

## LIVY

# A Slave Uprising in Apulia in 185 B.C.E.

### First Century B.C.E.

*The historian Livy (Documents 23–25) records a revolt in southern Italy connected with slave shepherds.*

In this year, there was a great slave uprising in Apulia. The praetor Lucius Postumius was assigned the province of Tarentum. He conducted judicial inquiries into a conspiracy of herdsmen who had made the roads and the common pasturelands dangerous by their acts of banditry. He condemned about seven thousand men. Although many of them escaped, many others were punished.

Livy, *History of Rome,* 39.29.8–9.

## 29

## LIVY

# The Repression of Slave Shepherds
# and the Bacchanals in Southern Italy in 184 B.C.E.

### First Century B.C.E.

*The historian Livy, writing at the end of the first century B.C.E., records a Roman army commander, praetor, using armed force to repress an uprising of slave shepherds (Document 28).*

The praetor Lucius Postumius, to whom the province of Tarentum was assigned by lot, savagely repressed large-scale conspiracies of herdsmen

Livy, *History of Rome,* 39.41.6–7.

and diligently completed the judicial inquiries into the last elements of the Bacchanalian conspiracies. Many persons who had been cited but who had not shown up for their hearings or who had abandoned their bail were hiding in those regions of Italy. Some of these men whom Postumius arrested he pronounced guilty on the spot, while others he sent to the Senate at Rome, where Publius Cornelius had all of them thrown into prison.

# 30

## LIVY

## The Continued Repression of Slave Shepherds and Bacchanals in Southern Italy in 182 B.C.E.

### First Century B.C.E.

*The historian Livy records the continuing use of Roman armed forces (Documents 28–29) to put down a dangerous slave revolt in southern Italy.*

A formal investigation concerning the Bacchanalian troubles was given as an additional task to the praetor Lucius Duronius, to whom Apulia had been assigned by lot as his province. These were some remnants that, like seeds planted by the earlier evils, had already begun to manifest themselves in the previous year. But the judicial inquiries into them, rather than being concluded, had in fact only been begun by the praetor Lucius Pupius in the previous year [183 B.C.E.]. The Senate ordered the new praetor to extinguish the threat completely, so that it would not be able to spread more widely again for a second time.

Livy, *History of Rome,* 40.19.9–10.

# 5

# The First Sicilian Slave War, 135–132 B.C.E.

The first major slave war faced by the Roman Republic erupted in the center of the island of Sicily, the state's first overseas province. According to most accounts, the war began with a sudden outburst of violence in 135 B.C.E. in the city of Enna, the agricultural center of one of the richest agricultural plains on the island and also an important cult center of the goddess Demeter. A slave named Eunus led the initial outbreak, but the war also involved other smaller revolts, led by local slave leaders, in different parts of the island.

At first, the Roman military response to the rebellion was feeble. Only after several resounding defeats did Rome take the war more seriously and assign regular military forces under praetorian commanders to the island. The war lasted for about four years. In its aftermath, there was much recrimination and blame, mostly of a moral nature, both of the slave masters, whose excessive harshness toward their slaves was seen as a significant cause of the war, and of the Roman governors and military commanders for their corruption, incompetence, and inaction.

The main account of the war comes from a Greek historian named Diodorus Siculus ("the Sicilian"), whose home city was Agyrion, on the island of Sicily, just north of Enna. He eventually left Sicily to settle in the city of Rome, where he completed a forty-book general history of the world from the beginning of human civilization to 60 B.C.E. The principal source that Diodorus used for events in Sicily was probably an earlier history written by Posidonius. Only fifteen of Diodorus's books have survived; unfortunately, the books relevant to the events of the great slave wars in Sicily have been lost. Therefore, we have to rely for information on much later writers who compiled synopses of the original work.

Two men summarized Diodorus's account of the slave wars in Sicily — Photios and Constantine Porphyrogennetos. Photios was head (patriarch) of the Orthodox Church at Constantinople between the 850s and 880s C.E. He compiled a vast compendium of synopses of classical works, including Diodorus's *History.* Constantine Porphyrogennetos ruled the Byzantine Empire from 945 to 949 C.E. While emperor, he directed that a reference reader, or encyclopedia, of classical literary works be compiled for his use. We call this reader the *Excerpts of Constantine.*

Following are these two versions of Diodorus's original account. It is important to read both accounts. Although the main elements of the story appear in both versions, there are significant differences between the two. The second account contains nuances and incidents not found in the first (e.g., it contains a more detailed account of the kind daughter of the slave owner Damophilos) that offer insights into how the story was told and explained by historians of the time. Compare and contrast the content of the two versions, as well as the different perspectives, values, and emphases of the writers.

**31**

## DIODORUS SICULUS

# The First Slave War on the Island of Sicily: First Version

*First Century B.C.E.*

---

*The following account is the one preserved in the writings of the Byzantine patriarch Photios.*

---

The Sicilians had been prosperous and happy in every respect for a period of sixty years following the destruction of Carthage, when the slave war erupted among them for the following cause. Since the Sicilians were in a rush to acquire ever more goods for their extravagant lifestyles and were accumulating great wealth, they began to purchase very large numbers of slaves. They immediately placed brands and tattoos on the bodies of these slaves, whom they drove away in herds from

---

Diodorus Siculus, *Library of History,* 34/35.2.1–24 [= Photios, *Library,* 284–86b].

the slave traders. They used the young men among them as herders and put the others to whatever use seemed most appropriate to each. The masters were arrogant and harsh in their treatment of the slaves. Since they were convinced that the slaves deserved only minimum care, they gave them the least possible food and clothing. Most of the slaves were forced to provide for their own livelihood by becoming bandits. These bandit gangs were scattered around the countryside like detachments of soldiers. The result was that every place in Sicily was filled with murder.

The Roman governors of Sicily tried to prevent the growth of these gangs, but they did not dare to punish them because of the power and influence of the landowners who were the masters of the slave-bandits. The governors were forced to overlook the plundering of their own province. Most of the great landowners were Roman *equites* [see glossary]. Since these same men were also jurors in the cases against Roman governors who were arraigned on charges arising from the maladministration of their provinces, the Romans who served as governors greatly feared them.[1] The slaves, who were crushed by their hardships and suffering, and who were continually humiliated and beaten beyond all reason, were no longer able to endure their lot. So they began to congregate in groups here and there as the opportunity presented itself, and they began to discuss the possibility of revolt. Finally, they put their plans into action.

There was a Syrian slave, from the city of Apamea, who was owned by a man named Antigenes, a citizen of the city of Enna. This slave was a magician and a wonder-worker who claimed that he was able to predict future events from messages sent to him by the gods while he was asleep. Indeed, he was able to deceive many people because of this clever talent of his. From these small beginnings, he did not stop at reciting the prophetic messages that he had in his dreams, but he also claimed that he was able to see the gods themselves and to learn from them about events that were to take place in the future. Of the many things that he reputedly saw in his visions, some actually turned out to be true—quite by chance, of course. Since the predictions that did *not* occur were never challenged by anyone, while those things that did happen gained notoriety, this slave's fame and repute increased rapidly. His most striking performance was this: While in a state of ecstatic possession, he was able, by the use of some device, to produce fire and to

[1]Some modern historians believe that this is a mistake or an anachronism, based on the belief that *equites* did not have an important role in the courts that tried miscreant governors until well after the end of the first slave war.

breathe flames from his mouth. While in a trance, he would utter more prophecies about the things to come. He would do this by placing some embers into a hollow shell (or something like this) that was pierced at either end with a hole. Then, putting the shell into his mouth and blowing on the embers, he would cause sparks and then flames to burst out.

Before the outbreak of the revolt, this same slave claimed that the Syrian goddess had appeared to him and had foretold that he was to become king. He announced this news not only to those around him in general but even to his own master. The whole thing was treated as a big joke. At his banquets, Antigenes, the master of this slave, would lead the others along in this bit of light entertainment. Antigenes would introduce Eunus (for this was the wonder-worker's name) to his guests, and he would question Eunus closely about his forthcoming kingship and about how he would treat each of the diners who was present when he became king. Without a moment's hesitation, Eunus would give a full account of everything, including how moderately he would treat the slave masters. Then there was the whole elaboration of his wonder-working itself. The diners would burst into laughter. Some of them would select a tasty tidbit from the dinner table and present it to Eunus as a gift, at the same time telling him that when he became king, he should remember them for this act of generosity. Not only did this wonder-working performed by Eunus result in a genuine kingship, but the repayment of the favors that he received as a joke at these banquets was done not without the goodwill of genuine gratitude.

The origin of the whole slave rebellion was as follows. There was a certain Damophilos, a citizen of Enna, who was an exceedingly wealthy man, but one who had a rather arrogant character. He had maltreated his slaves beyond all tolerable limits. His wife, Megallis, competed with her husband in the punishment and general inhumane treatment of their slaves. Because of this maltreatment, the slaves were reduced to the level of wild beasts and began to plot with one another for rebellion and the murder of their masters. They went to Eunus and asked him if the gods supported their plans. Following his normal procedure, through the use of his wonder-working skills, Eunus confirmed that the gods were favorable and advised the slaves to undertake their plan at once. They immediately collected four hundred of their fellow slaves. Arming themselves with such weapons as were available at the moment, they fell on the city of Enna. Eunus led them, working his usual wonders by breathing smoke and fire out of his mouth. Breaking into the houses in the city, the rebel slaves instituted a general slaughter, not even sparing the suckling infants among the inhabitants. Tearing them from their mothers' breasts, they dashed the infants to the ground. One cannot actually say in words what they did to the women themselves—and with their husbands looking on—what terrible acts of outrage and utter lewdness were committed on them.

A large number of slaves from the city now joined the rebels. The slaves first inflicted extreme savageries on their own masters, and then they turned to the slaughter of the rest of the inhabitants. When the slaves who were following Eunus learned that Damophilos was staying with his wife in a suburban villa near the city, they dispatched some of their own men to bring back the man and his wife in chains. They did so, subjecting the pair to repeated physical assaults on the way. Only in the case of their daughter did the slaves show any consistent care and consideration. In her case, they acted differently, because she had a kind and benevolent character. As far as was possible, she had always been sympathetic to the slaves and had tried to offer them help when any of them was in need. From these actions of theirs, it is shown that the violence of the slaves did not stem from an innate disposition toward others, but rather that their actions were only fair repayment for the injustices that had formerly been inflicted on them.

The men who had been dispatched to arrest Damophilos and Megallis and to bring them back to the city (as I have said) arraigned them both in the theater, where a great popular assembly of the rebels had convened. Damophilos tried to use various rhetorical maneuvers in an attempt to save himself and was actually beginning to convince some of the crowd with his arguments. But Hermeias and Zeuxis, men embittered against him in their attitudes, shouted out that he was a deceiver. Not being able to await the final decision of the people, the one man drove his sword through Damophilos's chest, while the other cut his throat with an ax. Next, Eunus was chosen king, not because of his courage or for his abilities as a military commander, but solely because of his wonder-working powers, since he was the one who had started the revolt and because his very name seemed to be a good omen that portended his kindly disposition to his new subjects.

Once he was made master of all the rebels, Eunus summoned a popular assembly and decreed that all the inhabitants of Enna who had been taken prisoner were to be executed, except for those who had some skill in the manufacture of weapons. These latter persons he put in chains and set to work in workshops. He gave Megallis to the female slaves to do with as they wished. When they had finished torturing her, they threw Megallis off a nearby cliff. Eunus killed his own masters, Antigenes and Pytho. Crowning his head with a diadem and adorning

**Figure 4.** *Coin Issued by the Rebel Slave Leader Eunus, a.k.a. Antiochus*
This coin features a veiled head of the goddess Demeter (or perhaps that
of Matêr, who was venerated by the slaves), with a stalk of wheat, the
most important agricultural product of the island. The legend Basi(leos)
Antio(chou) translates as "[coin of] King Antiochus," the title under which
Eunus proclaimed his new power. In striking this coin, the minters were
imitating a standard motif found on coins issued by the Greek city-state
of Enna. The rebel slaves were in effect advertising their autonomy as a
state.
E. S. G. Robinson, "Antiochus, King of the Slaves," *Numismatic Chronicle,*
vol. 20 (1920), pp. 175–76, fig. p. 175.

himself with all of the other accoutrements and symbols of kingship, he
declared his partner to be his queen. She was also a Syrian, a woman
who came from the same city as Eunus. He appointed as royal counselors those who seemed outstanding in their intelligence. Among them
was one Achaios—"Achaian" both by name and by ethnic origin—a
man who excelled in both planning and action.

As well as he was able, within three days Eunus had provided arms
for more than six thousand men, in addition to his other followers who
were armed with axes, hatchets, slings, sickles, fire-hardened spears,
and even cooking spits. In this fashion, Eunus moved about with his
forces, ravaging the countryside [around Enna]. When he had collected
a huge number of slaves, he became bold enough to engage in combat
with Roman field commanders. When he joined battle with them, Eunus
frequently came out the winner because of his larger numbers—he
now had more than ten thousand soldiers under his command.

While these events were taking place, a man named Kleon, a Cilician,
began a revolt of other slaves on the island. Everyone hoped that the

two groups of rebellious slaves would clash with each other in battle and that the rebels would destroy each other, thereby freeing Sicily of the uprising. But contrary to all expectations, the two groups merged their forces. Kleon subordinated himself wholly to Eunus's command and assumed the role of a general in the service of a king. Kleon had five thousand soldiers of his own. It was now almost thirty days after the outbreak of the revolt.

A short time later, the Roman commander, the praetor Lucius Hypsaeus, arrived from Rome. He had 8,000 soldiers recruited in Sicily under his command. When the two sides confronted each other on the battlefield, however, the rebels emerged victorious, since they now numbered 20,000. Not long afterward, their total collective strength reached 200,000. Consequently, they emerged victorious from many battles with the Romans; only infrequently did they come off the worse. When news of these events spread outside Sicily, a slave rebellion involving 150 conspirators broke out in Rome. Another one that involved more than a thousand slaves broke out in Attica, another occurred on the island of Delos, and more revolts broke out in many other places. Because of the speed with which help arrived and the severity with which punishment was inflicted, the men who were in charge of each community quickly put down these rebellions. This brought any others who were contemplating rebellion to their senses. In Sicily, however, the evils only grew in scale. Whole cities were besieged and captured along with their inhabitants. Many armies were completely destroyed by the rebels.

The situation changed only when the consul [Publius] Rupilius saved Tauromenium for the Romans by placing it under a close siege and encircling it so that the rebels were compelled to live in unspeakable conditions and famine. The besieged were reduced to such extremes, in fact, that they began first to eat their own children and then their women. Finally, in despair, they did not even shrink from devouring each other. It was on this occasion that Rupilius captured Kleon's brother Komanos [or Komas] when he was trying to escape from the besieged city. In the end, a Syrian named Sarapion betrayed the citadel, and the Roman commander was able to capture all the fugitive slaves in the city. When Rupilius had finished torturing the prisoners, he had them thrown off a high precipice.

From Tauromenium, Rupilius advanced to Enna, which he placed under a similar siege. By forcing the rebels into extremely dire straits, he finally broke their hope. Kleon, their commander, sallied forth from the city with a few men, fought heroically, and in the end died, his body covered with wounds. His corpse was put on public display. Rupilius captured this city by the same type of betrayal that he used at Tauromenium, since, because of the great strength of its fortifications, it could not be taken by ordinary force of arms.

Eunus took his bodyguard of a thousand men with him and, in a cowardly fashion, sought refuge in steep and rugged terrain. Since the Roman commander Rupilius was already marching against them in full force, the men who accompanied Eunus realized how defenseless they were against the impending disaster. Anticipating their fate, they cut each other's throats with their swords. The wonder-worker and king, Eunus, who, like a coward, had sought refuge in some caves, was dragged out along with four men—his cook, his baker, his bath masseur, and the master of entertainments at his drinking parties. After he had been placed in detention, his body was destroyed by a mass of lice,[2] as befits a man of his connivance. He ended his life at Morgantina.

Rupilius then scoured the whole of Sicily with crack troops that he divided into small operational units. In this way, he freed the island from the scourge of banditry much more quickly than had been expected.

Eunus, the king of the rebels, called himself "Antiochus" and his mob of rebels "Syrians."

---

[2]This was a typical death of tyrannical rulers, including Antiochus IV, Herod the Great, and the Roman emperor Galerius, who persecuted Christians. Plutarch provides a vivid, if not repellent, description of the death of the Roman strongman Lucius Cornelius Sulla in 78 B.C.E., when the ex-dictator's body turned into a mass of lice. Plutarch comments: "If we must make note of those men who were famous for other reasons, but who were not good men themselves, it is reported that the leader of the war of the runaway slaves in Sicily, called Eunus, was taken to Rome after his capture and died there of this lice-consuming disease" (*Life of Sulla,* 36).

## 32

## DIODORUS SICULUS

# The First Slave War on the Island of Sicily: Second Version

### First Century B.C.E.

---

*This is the account preserved in the Byzantine emperor Constantine Porphyrogennetos's* Excerpts. *Surviving only in fragments, this version of the slave rebellion covers the same sequence of events as the previous one, but it has different emphases and contains episodes not mentioned in the first account.*

---

Never had there been such a great uprising of slaves as then arose in Sicily. Because of it, cities fell into terrible disasters, and countless men and women, along with their children, experienced the gravest misfortunes. The whole island seemed about to fall into the hands of fugitive slaves, who measured the extent of their power by the excesses of the misfortunes that were suffered by free persons. These events struck the majority of people on the island suddenly and contrary to all expectation, but to those who could judge these events realistically, they did not seem to happen without good reason. Because of the excessive success and wealth of those who were taking profits from this exceedingly prosperous island, at first all of those who had become wealthy so quickly desired only a luxurious life. Later, however, they became arrogant and were filled with violent excesses. Since the maltreatment of the slaves increased in equal proportion to their alienation from their masters, when the first opportunity presented itself, there was a sudden violent outburst of hatred on the part of the slaves. The result was that, without any communication between themselves, tens of thousands of slaves joined forces to kill their masters. Almost the identical thing happened in Asia at the same time, when Aristonicus claimed the kingship

---

that was not rightly his.[1] Because their masters had treated them so terribly, the slaves in Asia joined Aristonicus and were the cause of great disasters to many unfortunate cities.

In almost the same fashion, each of the large landowners purchased entire lots of slaves to farm their lands. . . . *[The manuscript is defective.]* Some of them were shackled by their feet, others were ground down by the sheer weight of their work, but all of them had their bodies inscribed with the slave owners' arrogant marks of identification. Such large numbers of slaves flooded all of Sicily that those who heard the extravagant numbers involved would not believe them. The Sicilians themselves had now become so massively wealthy that they began to rival the Italians in their arrogance, in their greed for more, and in their wicked machinations. The Italians, who also owned large numbers of slaves, had already made their slave herdsmen so accustomed to the loose controls over them that the slave owners did not need to provide the slaves with any of the necessary supplies for living, but rather simply allowed them to engage in acts of banditry. Great power had been permitted to men who, because of their physical strength, were capable of doing anything they wished and who were fortunate to have free time on their hands. Since these men lacked even the basic necessities of life, they were driven to commit dangerous and risky acts. This quickly produced a rapid escalation of lawlessness.

At first, they murdered men who happened to be traveling alone or in pairs along the roads in out-of-the-way places. Then they gathered in gangs to attack the houses of unprotected people during the night, taking by force all their possessions and killing all those who tried to resist them. Finally, their daring became greater and greater, with the result that at night no road in Sicily was safe anymore. For those people who had been accustomed to living in the countryside, it was no longer safe to remain there. Every place was filled with violence, banditry, and every kind of murder. Since the slave herdsmen were raised in the rugged countryside and were armed like soldiers, naturally they were filled with arrogance and daring. They brandished clubs, spears, and imposing herdsmen's staffs, and their bodies were covered in the hides of wolves and wild boars, so that they had a frightening appearance that was not

---

[1]Aristonicus, who professed to have a legitimate claim to the throne of the kingdom of Pergamum, led an abortive rebellion at the time of King Attalus Ill's death in 133 B.C.E. He issued his own coinage as a symbolic assertion of his royal authority and appealed to the lower orders, including the slaves, for support. The Roman consul Marcus Perperna brought his revolt to a violent end in 129. Aristonicus was taken to Rome as a prisoner and executed there.

far from the savageries of war itself. Following close on the heels of each man was a pack of fierce dogs, while a regular diet of milk and raw meat made the bodies and minds of the men themselves thoroughly savage.

The whole island became filled with armed gangs scattered about the countryside, since, thanks to the permissiveness of their owners, the aggressive impulses of the slaves were now provided with the necessary weapons. The Roman governors tried to prevent the madness of the slaves, but they did not dare to punish them, because the authority and power of the slave masters forced the governors to look the other way while the province was being plundered by the bandits. The fact is that most of the landowners were well known Roman *equites*. Since these same men were judges in legal cases filed against the governors, arising from the maladministration of their provinces, they were greatly feared by the governors.[2]

The Italians who were beginning to engage in agricultural enterprises in Sicily purchased large numbers of slaves. They placed identifying marks on the slaves' bodies, but they did not provide them with sufficient food and ground them down with a brutal and oppressive work regime . . . and the enduring of these miseries. . . . *[The manuscript is defective.]*

Not only in the public realm of power should those in superior positions treat those who are humble and lowly with consideration. But similarly, in their private lives, if they understand their own situations accurately, they should treat their slaves considerately. Just as arrogance and brutal treatment in states leads to social upheaval and civil strife among the freeborn citizens, in the same way maltreatment produces plots against the masters by the slaves within the household. From this same source, fearsome rebellions are plotted against the state itself. To the degree that cruelty and lawlessness pervert the basic elements of power, to that same degree the characters of subject persons are made savage to the point of despair. For every person who has been made humble by chance or fate and who has willingly treated his superiors with goodness and respect, but who has been deprived of the expected humane consideration in return, will become an enemy to those who savagely lord it over him.

There was a certain Damophilos, born in Enna, who was an exceedingly wealthy man, but of arrogant character, who farmed a great circuit of lands filled with herds of cattle. He emulated the lifestyle of the Italians in Sicily—both in the great number of slaves that he possessed and in the inhumane and harsh way in which he treated them.

---

[2]See the note on page 75 concerning this claim about the status of the landowners and its supposed effect on the behavior of the Roman governors.

Damophilos used to go the rounds of his lands in four-wheeled coaches drawn by richly caparisoned[3] horses and accompanied by a retinue of armed slaves. In addition to these men, Damophilos also boasted a large number of handsome slave boys and a following of his favorites. Both in the city and in his rural villas, he displayed finely chased[4] silver vessels and purple-dyed coverings, and he had royal tables set with lavish feasts.

Damophilos exceeded even the luxuries of the Persians in his great outlays and expenditures. He also exceeded the Persians in arrogance. The command of a power that was answerable to no one and of a great wealth that was acquired by good luck affected Damophilos's uneducated and unschooled character. At first, his excessive wealth produced a desire only for what would suffice, but then it led to a violent impulse to acquire more, and finally to disaster and death for himself and to great misfortunes for his community.

Whenever he purchased a large number of slaves, Damophilos would treat them violently, inscribing letters and marks with instruments of iron on the bodies of men who had been freeborn citizens in their own lands, but who had suffered the fate of slavery through capture in warfare. Some of these he bound with leg irons and threw into slave barracks. Others he appointed to be his herdsmen, but these he did not provide with sufficient clothing or food.

When Damophilos of Enna was approached by some naked slaves who wished to speak with him about the matter of adequate clothing, he would not listen to their petition but said, "What's this? Men wandering around the countryside, parading in the nude? Why don't they just importune a theatrical patron to provide them with the cloaks that they need so badly?" He ordered them to be bound to pillars and beaten, and then he haughtily had them dismissed.

Because of the stubbornness and cruelty of his character, there was not a day on which Damophilos did not punish some of his slaves, and never for any just cause. And his wife Metallis,[5] who delighted no less in these excessive punishments, treated her women servants cruelly, as well as any of the other slaves who happened to cross her path. Because of the beatings and punishments administered by these two owners, their slaves became violently enraged toward them, and considering that nothing worse would happen to themselves than they were presently suffering. . . . *[The manuscript ends.]*

---

[3]*caparisoned:* adorned.
[4]*chased:* ornamented.
[5]Megallis in the first account.

The slaves began to plot with one another about a rebellion and the murder of their masters. They approached Eunus, who lived not far from them, and asked him if their plans had the approval of the gods. Eunus fell into a trancelike state and began working his wonders. When he heard why they had come, Eunus made clear to them that the gods favored their revolt as long as they did not delay too long but put their plans quickly into action. It had been foretold, he said, that Enna, the chief city of the whole island, was to be their homeland. When they heard his words, they were confident that the divine was with them in their revolt. Their spirits were so fired up for rebellion that they would accept no delay in the accomplishment of their aims. They immediately set loose those slaves who were in bonds. Then, collecting as many of the other slaves as happened to live nearby, they gathered together about four hundred men in a field that was close to Enna. Making pacts and forging bonds of trust with each other by swearing oaths over sacrifices in the middle of the night, they armed themselves as well as they could on the spur of the moment. They all donned the most powerful weapon of all: a rage that was directed at the destruction of their arrogant and overbearing masters. Eunus led them in their assault. Shouting encouragement to each other, the slaves burst into the city in the middle of the night and slaughtered many people.

The daughter of Damophilos, a girl approaching the age of marriage, simple in her character and remarkable for her human kindness, also lived in Sicily. She always showed concern for the slaves who were being beaten by her parents and felt sympathy for the ones that had been put in chains. Because of her kindness, she was greatly loved by everyone. So it happened in the present circumstances that her previous favors provoked in response the sympathy of those who had been treated well by her. Not only did no slave dare violently and shamefully to lay hands on the girl, but all of them made sure that the flower of her beauty was kept free from any outrage against her honor. Instead, the slaves selected the best men from their own numbers—the most outstanding among them was a man named Hermeias—and had them escort her safely to the home of some of her relatives in the city of Catana.

Although the rebellious slaves were wild with rage against all the households of their masters and resorted to uncontrolled violence and vengeance against them, it was clear that this response was not rooted in any innately savage nature. Rather, it was because of the outrages that had previously been committed against them that they now ran wild in the punishment of those who had previously done wrong to them. Even among slaves, human nature is perfectly capable of being its own teacher about what is just repayment, whether it be gratitude or vengeance.

After Eunus was hailed as king, he had all of them [the slave masters] killed, with the sole exception of those who in earlier times had deigned to invite him to their banquets when his master had allowed, men who had treated him kindly, who had shown respect for his prophetic powers, and who had given gifts of food to him from their own tables. Here was an amazing thing: a sudden shift in fortune and the fact that a favor granted for such a small thing should be repaid with such a great gift and at such a critical time.

Achaios, the personal adviser of King Antiochus [the slave leader Eunus's new royal name], was not pleased with the actions of the runaway slaves and reprimanded them for the outrages they were committing. He announced, with some bravado, that they would suffer immediate punishment for these acts. Not only did Eunus not put Achaios to death for his use of free speech, but he gave him the house of his former masters as a gift and made him one of his royal counselors.

There was another revolt of runaway slaves on the island worthy of record. Kleon, a Cilician from the region of the Taurus Mountains, had been accustomed to a life of banditry from the time he was a small child. In Sicily, he became a herder of horses and a man who habitually robbed travelers and committed murders all over the place. When he learned of Eunus's success and of the victories of the fugitive slaves under his command, he decided to lead his own revolt. He persuaded some of the slaves close by to join his mad enterprise. They overran the city of Acragas and almost all of the surrounding countryside.

Their pressing needs and lack of resources forced the rebel slaves to have a good opinion of everyone; they did not have the luxury of selecting only the stronger and better men.

There was no need of some heaven-sent sign to make them realize that the city was open to capture. Even to the dullest person, it was clear that the city's walls had fallen into disrepair because of the prolonged peaceful conditions and that now, when many of its soldiers had been killed, it was easily exposed to a successful siege.

Eunus had stationed his forces outside the range of the catapult bolts. He cursed the Romans, shouting out that it was not his men but the Romans who were the real fugitives—in their case, from the dangers of war. He even staged dramatic mime performances for the people inside the city on the theme of the slave rebellion—dramas in which the slaves themselves acted out the events of their rebellion against their masters. In these dramatic skits, the slaves poured contempt on the arrogance and outrageous insolence that had led to the slave owners' self-destruction.

As for sudden and unexpected blows of misfortune, there are those who are persuaded that the divine has nothing at all to do with such occurrences. Yet, even so, it is surely to the advantage of the common good of society that fear of the gods should be inculcated in the minds of the great majority of ordinary people. For those who do the right thing because of their personal moral excellence are few in number. The vast majority of humankind refrain from doing wrong only because of the penalties exacted by the laws and the punishments coming from the gods.

When these great and countless evils were inflicted on the people of Sicily, the democratic mob had no sympathy when they witnessed the misfortunes of the slave masters. Quite the opposite: They were overjoyed. The common people were filled with envy because of their unequal share in the community and because of the lives they were compelled to lead, so very different from those of the rich. This envy of theirs, caused by the suffering that I have mentioned, turned to joy when they saw that the resplendent lot of the rich had been reduced to depths that would once have been beneath the contempt of even ordinary citizens. But what was the most terrible of all was the fact that the rebel slaves, who at least had some reasonable forethought, did not set fire to the rural villas of the rich and did not destroy the goods and harvests that were stored on the country estates of the wealthy. Indeed, in general they refrained from doing harm to anyone involved in farming. The free common people, however, used the runaway slaves as an excuse. Rushing out into the countryside, they not only pillaged and plundered the possessions of the rich, but they also set fire to their country villas—all out of envy.

The runaway Syrian slaves cut off the hands of their prisoners. Not satisfied with cutting off the hands alone, however, amid these terrible mutilations they made it their practice to cut off the whole of the person's arm.

Those persons who ate the sacred fish[6] suffered many evils. The divine force, as if displaying what was fitting as an example for the others, left all of those who had acted with so little consideration with no relief from these ills. These same people, in accordance with the vengeance inflicted by the gods, have also received blame in our historical accounts and so have reaped the kind of just punishment they deserve.

Since the Senate was struck with a reverent fear of the divine, it dispatched an embassy to Sicily in accordance with a Sibylline oracle [see glossary]. The ambassadors went to visit all the altars that had been established for Aetnean Zeus throughout the island of Sicily and made sacrifices at

[6]*sacred fish:* Probably the fish sacred to the goddess Artemis that were kept in a pond at the fountain of Arethusa in Syracuse. Such fish also were central to the worship of the Syrian goddess Atargatis, and so they were probably well known to the rebel slaves.

these altars. They also had barriers erected around the altars and ordered that no one was to have access to them except for those political communities that had by tradition made ancestral sacrifices at each particular place.

There was a man from Morgantina, one Gorgos, who was also known as Kambalos, a man who was preeminent in his wealth and personal reputation. One day he was out on the chase with his hunting dogs, when by chance he ran into a bandit gang of runaway slaves. To escape them, he began to run back to the city on foot. His father, Gorgos, who was out riding on horseback, happened to encounter his son. He dismounted and offered his son the horse so that the son might save himself by riding back to the city. The son, however, would not put his own safety before that of his father; nor was the father willing to accept the death of his son by making his own escape from the impending danger. As they were tearfully pleading with each other and contending with each other in respect and affection—the virtue of a parent's love for a child contesting with the son's love for a father—the bandits caught up with them and murdered them both.

The documents that follow are minor sources for the first slave war on Sicily. They are often synopses, brief asides, and other snippets of information contained in histories, letters, and speeches from later times. Although often tangential to the main concerns of the writers, these pieces of information might confirm the general outline of the events described in the previous two accounts or add details that would otherwise be unknown.

# 33

## LIVY

# A Brief Summary of the Main Events of 136–129 B.C.E.

### First Century B.C.E.

*The historian Livy records the continuing use of Roman armed forces (Documents 28–29) to put down a dangerous slave revolt in southern Italy.*

A slave war erupted in Sicily. Since the praetors were not able to suppress it, the consul Gaius Fulvius [Flaccus] [134 B.C.E.] was ordered to

Livy, *Summaries*, 56, 58–59.

take the field. The man who caused this war was a slave named Eunus, a man of Syrian origin. Eunus collected a force of rural slaves, broke open the slave barracks, and in this way raised the numbers of his men to those of a regular army. Another slave, named Cleon [Kleon], likewise gathered together about seventy thousand slaves. After these two men joined forces, they fought several battles against the Roman army.
. . . [This book] includes, in addition, an account of the campaigns in Sicily that were undertaken against the fugitive slaves, although with varying degrees of success.

Publius Rupilius, the consul [in 132 B.C.E.], brought the war against the fugitive slaves in Sicily to an end. Aristonicus, the son of the king Eumenes, took possession of Asia, although according to the last will and testament of King Attalus in which his kingdom was bequeathed to the Roman people, it was to be a free state. Publius Licinius Crassus, the consul [in 131 B.C.E.], although he was also pontifex maximus [see glossary] (a thing that had never happened before), actually left the land of Italy to attack Aristonicus. He was defeated in battle and died. Marcus Perperna, the consul, defeated Aristonicus and received his surrender.

**34**

**JULIUS OBSEQUENS**

*The Slave War in Sicily and Contemporary Slave Rebellions in Italy in 134–132 B.C.E.*

*Fifth Century C.E.*

---

*Julius Obsequens collected "prodigies," or unusual occurrences of religious significance, mainly from the text of the historian Livy. From these we learn of slave revolts that took place in Italy at the same time as the first slave war in Sicily.*

---

In the year that Publius Africanus and Gaius Fulvius [Flaccus] were consuls [134 B.C.E.]:

Outbreak of the war against the fugitive slaves in Sicily. A conspiracy of slaves in Italy was repressed.

---

Julius Obsequens, *Book of Prodigies,* 27, 27b.

In the year that Pubillius Popillius and Publius Rupilius were consuls [132 B.C.E.]:

In Italy many thousands of slaves who had formed a conspiracy were suppressed, but with difficulty, and were exterminated by punishment. In Sicily, fugitive slaves slaughtered Roman armies.

## 35

### OROSIUS

# The Slave War in Sicily and Contemporary Slave Rebellions in Italy and Greece

### Fifth Century C.E.

*This abbreviated account of the slave war in Sicily and similar slave uprisings elsewhere in the Mediterranean comes from the history of Orosius, who was probably preserving much of what was once in Livy.*

In the year in which Servius[1] Fulvius Flaccus and Quintus Calpurnius Piso were consuls [135 B.C.E.], there was born to a slave woman at Rome a boy with four feet, four hands, four eyes, double the usual number of ears, and two sets of sexual organs. In Sicily, Mount Aetna erupted in great flashes of fire and poured out lava that rushed like flash floods down its slopes. Objects close to the volcano were completely burned by the fires, while those more distant were scorched by the burning ashes that were scattered far and wide, along with poisonous gases. The portent signaled by this volcano, in a phenomenon that was always peculiar to Sicily, did not so much proclaim a forthcoming evil as it actually caused one to happen. . . .

As a result, a slave war broke out in Sicily. Because of the large numbers of slaves involved, and because of their equipment and supplies,

---

[1]Orosius is mistaken about the consul's first name. It should be Gaius.

Orosius, *History against the Pagans,* 5.6.1–6, 5.9.4–8.

this war was both serious and savage. The war utterly destroyed Roman praetors and struck terror even into consuls. Of the conspirators who were in arms, they say that the total number of slaves reached seventy thousand men. This total, however, does not include the slaves of the city of Messana. Since they had been treated fairly, they remained peaceful. In any event, the situation in Sicily was worse because it was an island and it never had an independent law of its own, but was at some times subject to tyrants and at other times to slaves. The tyrants exacted slavery by their evil domination of others, and the slaves, by their perverse arrogance, brought about the inversion of freedom and servitude. Furthermore, since Sicily is closed off on all sides by the sea, its internal troubles cannot easily be dissipated abroad. Sicily, indeed, nourished a viper conceived for its own destruction, a viper that grew very large because of Sicily's compulsive lusts and was destined to live at the cost of Sicily's destruction. Inasmuch as it is a rare kind of uprising, an insurrection of slaves is a more dangerous type of rebellion: Masses of free citizens are prompted by their aims to increase the strength of their homeland, whereas a mob of slaves is incited to destroy it. . . .

What is more, the contagious disease of the Sicilian slave war infected many provinces far and wide. At Minturnae [in Italy], 450 slaves were crucified. At Sinuessa, an uprising of about 4,000 slaves was crushed by Quintus Metellus [consul in 143 B.C.E.] and Gnaeus Servilius Caepio [praetor in 143 B.C.E.]. A revolt of slaves in the mines at Athens was repressed by the "praetor" Heraclitus.[2] On the island of Delos, slaves who were about to break out in a new revolt were repressed by the preemptive actions taken by the citizens of the island. All of these other incidents were caused by the first source of this evil in Sicily, which scattered the embers, so to speak, that sparked the other fires. The consul Piso, who succeeded Fulvius as commander in Sicily, captured the town of the Mamertines [i.e. modern Messana], where he killed 8,000 fugitive slaves. Those whom he was able to capture alive, he nailed to crosses. In turn, he was succeeded by the consul Rutilius [Rupilius], who recaptured Tauromenium and Enna, which had been the most strongly fortified of the refuges held by the fugitive slaves. They say that more than 20,000 slaves were slaughtered in these operations. The

---

[2]*Heraclitus:* He was not actually a Roman praetor, but rather a local official of the city-state of Athens.

causes of this great and protracted war were certainly lamentable. The slave masters were bound to lose everything unless they opposed their increasingly insolent slaves with the blade of a sword. And yet, as far as the tragic destruction caused by the fighting and the unhappy rewards of victory were concerned, the victors themselves lost just as much as the defeated.

# 36

## POSIDONIUS

### The Cause of the Slave War

#### First Century B.C.E.

*Posidonius, a Greek polymath in the first century B.C.E., shared his views on what had caused the first Sicilian slave war.*

In the eighth book of his *Histories,* Posidonius says concerning Damophilos the Sicilian, the man who was the cause of the slave war: He was a slave of luxury and evildoing. He traveled through the countryside in four-wheeled carriages drawn by splendid horses and was accompanied by an escort of handsome young slaves, parasites, and a coterie of boys in livery. Later, however, he and his whole family met their end in a suitably humiliating manner, the object of his own slaves' contempt.

Posidonius, *Histories* [Kidd-Edelstin, F59; Jacoby, *FGrH,* F7: from Athenaeus, *Deipnosophistae,* 12.542b].

## 37

## APPIAN

# The Tribune of the Plebs on the Dangers Posed by the Slave War in Sicily

### Second Century *C.E.*

*In this brief passage, the historian Appian writes about the demands made by Tiberius Gracchus, the tribune of the plebs in 133 B.C.E., for a redistribution of public land to Roman citizens. In making his arguments in support of a strong freeborn citizen body of farmers, Tiberius Gracchus was careful to point out the deleterious effects of slavery.*

Tiberius was very critical of the large numbers of slaves in Italy as useless for warfare and of the slaves themselves as disloyal to their owners. He pointed to the recent disaster inflicted by the slaves on their masters in Sicily, precisely in a situation where the demands of agriculture had greatly increased their numbers. He also brought to mind the war waged against these slaves by the Romans, a war that was neither easy to win nor short in duration. Rather, it had been a protracted conflict that was dangerous and filled with unexpected shifts in fortune.

Appian, *Roman History: The Civil Wars,* 1.9.36.

## 38

## CICERO

# The Behavior of the Rebel Slaves at Enna

### First Century *B.C.E.*

*In his prosecution of Gaius Verres, the former Roman governor of Sicily who was brought to trial on charges of extortion in 70 B.C.E., the Roman*

Cicero, *Against Verres,* 2.4.112.

*orator and senator Cicero purposefully maligned Verres' behavior by
making his actions in Sicily seem even worse than those of the rebel
slaves. For Cicero's prosecution of Verres, see Documents 74 and 75.*

Was it from Enna that you [Gaius Verres] dared to take away the statue
of Ceres [Demeter]? Was it at Enna that you tried to snatch the statue of
the goddess Victory from the hand of Ceres, thus robbing one goddess
from the other? You did this, when even those men [the rebel slaves],
whose very being was that of wickedness rather than piety, desisted
from desecrating or indeed even touching these holy objects? In the
consulship of Publius Popil[l]ius and Publius Rupilius [132 B.C.E.], this
place was occupied by slaves—runaways, savages, and public enemies.
Yet these men were less the slaves of their masters than you are the
slave of your lusts. They were less fugitives from their masters than you
are from what is lawful and right. They were less savage by speech and
origin than you are by birth and character. They were less the enemies
of humanity than you are of the gods.

# 39

## STRABO

## *The Devastation of Sicily*

### *First Century C.E.*

*In the geographer Strabo's description of Sicily, written about a century
after the end of the second slave war on the island, he reports on the long-
term effects of the slave wars on Sicily's economy and settlement.*

Very few people live in the city of Enna in the hinterland [of the island
of Sicily], where the temple of Demeter is located. Enna is situated on
a high crest of land. Lying all around it are high mountain plains, all of
them rich and arable. The city suffered severely when the fugitive slaves
led by Eunus were besieged and, only with great difficulty, were forced

Strabo, *Geography,* 6.2.6–7.

out of the city by the Romans. The people of Catana and Tauromenium, and very many other cities, also suffered from these same problems.

*[At this point, Strabo describes the town of Eryx, the temple of Venus Erycina, and the temple slaves who served this complex.]*

All of the other settlements in the hinterland have, for the greatest part, been given over to herdsmen. I do not know of any persons living at Gela or Kallipolis or Selinus or Euboea or at many of the others. . . . The Romans, realizing that the land was deserted, took possession of the highlands and most of the plains regions and handed them over to men who herded horses, cattle, and sheep. Many times the island of Sicily fell into great dangers because of these men. At first, the herdsmen turned to banditry only sporadically, but later they began to operate in much larger numbers and pillaged the local settlements, as when Enna was seized by Eunus and his men.

More recently, in my own time, a man named Selouros was sent to Rome under arrest. He was nicknamed the "Son of Aetna" because he had led a gang of bandits that, for a long time, had overrun the lands around Mount Aetna, staging repeated hit-and-run raids on the surrounding settlements. I saw this man in gladiatorial games staged in the forum at Rome, where he was killed by being torn to pieces by wild beasts. Selouros was placed on a high contraption, as if he were on top of Mount Aetna. This tower was constructed in such a way that it would suddenly collapse into pieces. The result was that Selouros fell into the cages of the wild animals, which were built to fall open easily and had been constructed underneath the edifice for this purpose.

**40**

**FLORUS**

## The Extent of the Devastation of Sicily Caused by the Slaves

### Second Century C.E.

*The Latin author Florus seems to have depended mainly on the accounts of Livy and Sallust for his information on the slave wars. Since their*

Florus, *A Synopsis of Roman History,* 2.7.1–8.

*historical works on these wars have been lost, Florus's words, even if they*
*are only a shadowy summary of what once existed, are still useful.*

Even if we fought against our own Italian allies—itself an impious act—at least we fought with free and freeborn men. But who can even bear the thought, and not be greatly disturbed by it, of wars waged by slaves against the leading people of the civilized world? The first attempt at a slave war took place in the city of Rome itself, in the early years of its history, under the leadership of Herdonius the Sabine [460 B.C.E.]. On this occasion, when the city was occupied with the seditions caused by the tribunes of the plebs, the Capitolium[1] was seized, but it was later taken back by the consul. This incident, however, was more a civil insurrection than a genuine war.

Then [at a much later time], when our rule was established over very diverse and very distant lands, who could believe that Sicily would be far more cruelly devastated in a war fought against slaves than it had been by the war with the Carthaginians? This land, so rich in its production of cereal crops and, in a manner of speaking, almost a suburb of Rome, was divided into extensive agricultural domains that were owned by Roman citizens. The large numbers of slaves who worked lands owned by these men, and who were either housed in slave barracks or kept in chains, provided the basic manpower for the war.

A certain Syrian named Eunus—the very magnitude of the disasters he caused makes us remember him—by feigning a sort of crazed madness and tossing about his locks of hair in his worship of the Syrian goddess, incited the slaves to arms and to freedom, pretending that he had received such a command from the divine spirit. To prove that he was acting under divine inspiration, he hid in his mouth a hollow nutshell that he had filled with sulfur and embers, so that, by exhaling slowly, he breathed out flames while he spoke. This miracle initially attracted two thousand men from those whom he happened to meet, but later, when the slave barracks had been broken open by the right of war,[2] he assembled an army of more than sixty thousand.

Leaving no evil undone, Eunus even adorned himself with royal insignia. He inflicted a devastation on fortified places, villages, and towns that was pitiful to behold. Finally, in the ultimate shame of the war, he even captured the army camps of Roman praetors. But I am not ashamed to

---

[1] *Capitolium:* temple of Jupiter on the Capitoline hill in Rome.
[2] *right of war:* idea that one can do what one wishes in war.

name the commanders involved: They were Manlius, Lentulus, Piso, and Hypsaeus. The result was that praetorian commanders who ran from the battlefield were pursued by men who ought to have been arrested by professional hunters of runaway slaves. Finally, under the command of Perperna, punishment was inflicted on the fugitive slaves. For Perperna defeated their forces and, in the final event of the war, placed them under siege at Enna, where he destroyed them with a famine that was as lethal as any plague. Those bandits who survived he punished with leg irons, chains, and crucifixion. Perperna contented himself with an *ovatio* [see glossary] for his victory over the slaves, so that he would not besmirch the honor of a triumph [see glossary] by displaying a sign[3] that it was for vanquishing mere slaves.

# 41

## VALERIUS MAXIMUS

# Stories of Bravery and Cowardice of Romans and Slaves in the War

### First Century C.E.

*In the early first century C.E., Valerius Maximus produced a large collection of memorable sayings and accomplishments of famous persons. He intended these as examples to be imitated by his readers. Although they are not much more than moralizing vignettes, they preserve materials from other sources that have been lost.*

1. There once existed those men who were dedicated to military discipline even if this meant breaking the bonds of kinship and friendship. They did not hesitate to exact punishment for a wrong that had been committed, even if it meant shame for their own households. Thus, Publius Rupilius, when he was consul in the war that he fought in Sicily against the runaway slaves, ordered his son-in-law Quintus Fabius to

---

[3]*sign:* In the general's triumphal parade, inscribed banners and signs announced to the spectators who the defeated enemy were.

---

Valerius Maximus, *Memorable Deeds and Words,* 2.7.3, 2.7.9, 4.3.10, 6.9.8, 9.12.1.

leave the province when, because of his negligence, he lost the fortified position at Tauromenium.

*[The Latin text of the passage above is marked with textual difficulties.]*

2. The consul Lucius Calpurnius Piso [consul in 133 B.C.E.], when he was waging the war against the fugitive slaves, punished Gaius Titius, the commander of a cavalry unit, for having surrendered his arms when he was surrounded by enemy forces. Piso inflicted the following kinds of humiliating punishments on Titius. He ordered him to be dressed in a toga cut into tatters and covered with an unbelted tunic, and, through the whole period of his tour of duty, to stand in his bare feet from early morning to late at night in front of his [Piso's] headquarters. He forbade Titius to have any contact with the other men or to use the bath facilities. The consul also confiscated the horses of the cavalry unit that Titius had commanded and transferred the cavalrymen themselves to units of slingers. Although the humiliation suffered by our fatherland was great, an equal shame was suffered by the guilty. They were our soldiers who, simply because of their wish to live, had allowed fugitive slaves, worthy only of crucifixion, to erect trophies for their victories over us—free men who had not even blushed at being forced to pass under a shameful yoke made by slaves. Piso made these men feel the mere light of day in which they lived as bitter, so that those who had feared death like a bunch of women would now actually hope for it like real men.

3. By exemplifying the virtue of self-control, Calpurnius Piso was able to rival the Fabii and the Ogulnii[1] in glory. It is proven by the facts. When he was consul, Calpurnius Piso freed Sicily from the dangerous war with the fugitive slaves. According to army custom, Piso bestowed awards on those men whose extraordinary deeds had been of special use. Among the men who were singled out for honors was his own son, who, in holding certain specific positions, had fought very bravely. Piso awarded him a gold crown that was three pounds in weight, but only as an honorary title, declaring publicly that he considered it unfitting that a public official should expend funds of the state that would then enter the income of his own family. He therefore promised to leave the young man in his will an amount of gold equal to the gold in the crown. In this way, the honor would be bestowed publicly by the commander, while the son would receive the monetary part of the reward privately from his father.

4. As for Publius Rupilius, while he did not actually engage in taking tax-collection contracts for Sicily, he did do work for the private companies of tax collectors. In the same way, finding himself extremely

---

[1]*Fabii and Ogulnii:* two of the most illustrious political families of the early Roman Republic, whose heyday was in the third and second centuries B.C.E.

hard-pressed financially, he actually hired out his services to the allied cities in Sicily. A little while later, when he became consul, all the Sicilians received their laws from him, and he freed them from the savage war against bandits and fugitive slaves. Indeed, if there could be any feeling in mute objects, I think that the gates of the city themselves would be astonished at such a great change of status in the same individual. For they witnessed a man just getting by on his day-to-day income, while they later saw the same man dispensing the law and commanding naval fleets and armies.

5. There are even deaths of barbarians that are deserving of memory. One such death was that of a man named Komas [Komanos] who, it is said, was the brother of Kleon, the supreme commander of the bandits. When Roman forces retook Enna, which had up until then been held by the brigands, Komas was brought before the consul Publius Rupilius. When Komas was being questioned about the number of his men and what the fugitive slaves were trying to do, he paused and steeled himself. Komas covered his head, bent down on his knees, and held his breath until he died in the arms of the guards, right in front of the consul himself. Miserable and contemptible men, who would in fact be better off dead, torture themselves during their interrogation with the fear and the dread of the death that might happen to them and worry about the form that it might take. In their minds, they sharpen the iron blade, mix the required doses of poison, take a rope in their hands, or cast their eyes to the tops of precipitous cliffs—as if one needed great preparations and extraordinary efforts to bring the partnership between body and soul to an end. Komas needed none of this. He ended his own life by extinguishing the life in his own chest.

**42**

*Slingshot Ammunition Used by Roman Soldiers*
*133 B.C.E.*

*Just like modern bomber crews who painted slogans on the bombs they dropped, Roman soldiers who used slingshots as weapons frequently inscribed words on the "bullets" they used as ammunition. Sometimes these words were meant to encourage their own side—for example, the name of their commander. At other times, bullets were inscribed with crude obscenities, slurs, or curses aimed at the enemy.*

*Corpus Inscriptionum Latinarum*, vol. I², no. 847.

*The following example is an inscription from a slingshot bullet found in 1808 at Castrogiovanni in Sicily, near the site of ancient Enna. Many of these bullets have been discovered there, both on the heights of the site itself and on the surrounding slopes. Some bullets are inscribed; others are not. About thirty or so are inscribed with the Roman commander's name, as follows:*

## LUCIUS PISO, SON OF LUCIUS, THE CONSUL

*See also Document 55 for other examples of bullet inscriptions from the second slave war on Sicily.*

# 6

# The Second Sicilian Slave War, 104–100 B.C.E.

The second major slave war that afflicted the Roman state was almost a carbon copy of the first. Taking place a generation after the first war, it also occurred on the island of Sicily. The sequence of events and the actions of the main protagonists are so reminiscent of the first slave war that some modern historians have hypothesized that the Greek and Roman historians who told the story of the second war simply copied the narrative patterns of the first. The real differences between the two wars, however, are significant, and the similarities may be explained by imitative behavior—the slaves and their repressors had learned from the first great war—and by the similar social, economic, and geographic conditions in which the events happened.

The main difference between the first and second slave wars is in their causes. A series of events in the year 104 B.C.E. created a recruiting crisis for the Roman army. The need for manpower led to a demand for increased contributions to Roman forces from Rome's allies. When the king of Bithynia protested that he could not provide men on the scale demanded because large numbers of the men in his kingdom had been kidnapped and taken into slavery by slave traders, the Roman senate responded by passing a measure intended to protect people of free status in the provinces of the Roman Empire from being wrongfully detained as slaves. This decree raised expectations of freedom among many of the people already held in slavery on the island of Sicily—slaves who had a model for resistance in their social memory. The war that broke out in the eastern part of the island in 104 B.C.E. lasted for four years and, once again, seems to have succeeded in part because of Roman inaction. The sudden explosion of slave resistance appears to have taken the local landowning elite in Sicily and the Roman authorities by surprise. Our main account of the war is, once again, that preserved in the surviving fragments of the history composed by Diodorus Siculus ("the Sicilian"), who perhaps had some ancestral memories of the second slave war.

## 43

### DIODORUS SICULUS

# Events That Portended the Second Great Slave War: The Rebellion of Titus Vettius

## First Century B.C.E.

*Diodorus prefaced his account of the slave war with an account of an odd incident in southern Italy involving slaves who were incited to join a destitute young nobleman in an episode of local violence. Diodorus presents this strange episode as a sort of prefiguration of the more fearsome war that soon erupted on Sicily. The account survives in two slightly different versions.*

It was the time when [Gaius] Marius defeated the African kings Bocchus and Jugurtha in a great upheaval in North Africa, a war in which he killed many thousands of Africans and took Jugurtha prisoner. Bocchus had first seized Jugurtha, so that Bocchus received a pardon from the Romans for the fact that he had opposed them in the war. It was also the time when the despondent Romans had suffered a shocking series of military defeats at the hands of the Cimbri in Gaul. This was the same time when men from Sicily came to the city of Rome to report that a rebellion involving tens of thousands of slaves was taking place in their own homeland. When this news was announced, the whole Roman state was in a great crisis. Since almost sixty thousand enlisted men had been lost in the war against the Cimbri in Gaul, there was now a shortage of troops to be sent out on campaign against any new enemy.

Before the outbreak of the revolt of the slaves in Sicily, however, there occurred a number of brief, small-scale slave uprisings in Italy itself, as if the divine spirit were signaling in advance the magnitude

Diodorus Siculus, *Library of History,* 36.1.1–10.2 [= Photios, *Library,* 386–87b]; 36.2a.1–3 [= *Excerpts of Constantine,* 3, 208].

of the uprising that was about to take place in Sicily. The first of these minor rebellions occurred at Nuceria, where thirty slaves formed a conspiracy but were swiftly punished. The second uprising was at Capua, where two hundred slaves rebelled. They, too, were quickly repressed.

The third rebellion was a little odd. There was a man named Titus [Vettius] Minutius, who held the rank of *eques* [see glossary] and whose father was a man of great wealth. He fell in love with a slave girl, a woman of exceptional beauty, who happened to be owned by another man. Having had sex with her and fallen desperately in love, Minutius tried to purchase the girl for the sum of seven Attic talents,[1] so violently was he compelled by his mad love for the woman. With some difficulty, he was finally able to persuade the girl's master to agree to this plan. A date was set by which Minutius was to pay off the debt, since he had been extended credit on the basis of his father's wealth. When the day arrived and he did not have the means to pay what he owed, a new deadline of thirty days was set. When this day also arrived and the creditors asked for payment, Minutius did not have any more resources to meet the payment than he had had on the first occasion. Since he was still ablaze with love for the woman, he did something that was against all reason: He concocted plots against his creditors and began to claim the powers of a king.

Minutius acquired five hundred individual sets of armor and weaponry. He was advanced the credit to pay for these weapons and arranged for a delay in the payment. In secret, he stockpiled the arms in one of his fields and incited four hundred of his own slaves to open rebellion. Then he donned a diadem and a purple cloak, surrounded himself with lictors [see glossary] and other symbols of office, and with the support of his slaves appointed himself king. He had the creditors who had been demanding payment for the girl from him beaten with rods and then beheaded.

Minutius provided his slaves with full armament and began to make attacks on nearby rural estates. Those who eagerly joined his cause, he also provided with arms; those who opposed him, he had killed. Very quickly, he acquired a following of more than seven hundred men. Next, he enrolled them into regular military units and divided them into centuries.[2] Minutius then established these men in a palisaded fort and received with open arms anyone who was willing to join the rebellion.

When the rebellion was reported to Rome, the Senate sensibly took counsel concerning the uprising and instigated measures to repress it.

---

[1]About seventy to eighty times the usual price for a slave.
[2]Equivalent to regular fighting units of eighty to one hundred men in the Roman army.

Of the praetors who were then in the city, they appointed one, Lucius Lucullus, to the task of apprehending the fugitive slaves. On the very day that he was appointed, Lucullus conscripted 600 soldiers from the city of Rome. When he arrived at Capua, he summoned 4,000 infantry and 400 cavalry. When Vettius [Minutius] learned of Lucullus's impending attack, he occupied a strong rise in the land. By now, he had more than 3,500 men under his command.

At the first stage of the engagement, since they were fighting with the advantage of the higher ground, the fugitive slaves were able to beat back Lucullus's forces. By corrupting a man named Apollonius, who was acting as one of Vettius's commanders, and gaining his support with a formal promise of immunity from punishment, Lucullus was able to persuade the man to betray his fellow rebels. Now that he was cooperating with the Romans, Apollonius turned his forces against Vettius, who, fearing the punishment that he would suffer if he were taken prisoner, cut his own throat. The rest of the rebels followed his fate, except for the traitor Apollonius. These events transpired before the great slave rebellion that took place in Sicily, as if they were a foreshadowing of it.

# 44

## DIODORUS SICULUS

# The Second Slave War on the Island of Sicily: First Version

### First Century B.C.E.

*Like Diodorus's account of the first slave war on Sicily, his record of the second slave war has been preserved in two versions. Despite their apparent similarity, it is worth reading both accounts, since each contains some perspectives and facts not found in the other. This is the version preserved in the Byzantine patriarch Photios's* Library.

When the Senate assigned the command against the Cimbri to Marius, it gave him the right to request help from the overseas peoples of

Diodorus Siculus, *Library of History,* 36.3.1–10.2 [= Photios, *Library,* 387–90].

the empire according to their terms of alliance. It was in this context that Marius sent requests to Nicomedes, the king of Bithynia, to ask for his assistance. In his reply, Nicomedes stated that Roman government contractors had kidnapped the majority of Bithynian men and that they were now slaves in the provinces of the empire. The Senate then decreed that no person who was a free citizen of an allied state was to remain enslaved in a Roman province and that the governors of the provinces ought to take measures to see that such persons were set free. In compliance with this decree, Licinius Nerva, who was governor of Sicily at the time, established judicial hearings and immediately set about freeing slaves. Within a few days, more than eight hundred people obtained their freedom. The main consequence of these events was that all people who were in slavery on the island now had their eyes set on freedom.

The rich and the powerful on the island hurried to see the governor and urged him to refrain from pursuing this course of action. Whether persuaded by their money or enslaved by their patronage, Nerva showed no more interest in his judicial hearings. As a sort of punishment, he ordered those slaves who came to him seeking freedom to go back to their masters. These slaves then gathered together. Fleeing from the city of Syracuse, they took refuge in the sanctuary of the Palikoi.[1] There they began to debate with each other about rebellion. From this point on, the daring of the slaves became manifest in many places, but the first ones who made a strike for freedom were thirty slaves who belonged to two very wealthy brothers who lived in the countryside around Halicyae. A man named Varius led them. First, they cut their masters' throats at night while they were asleep. Then, rushing to the neighboring farms, they called the slaves on them to freedom. That same night their number rose to more than 120. Taking possession of a local place that was a natural strong point, the rebels made it even stronger, and they accepted into their number another 80 slaves who had armed themselves. Licinius Nerva made a quick march against them but had no success against the resistance of the besieged.

When force proved useless against the defensive position held by the slaves, the governor began to consider the instrument of betrayal. With promises of immunity, he persuaded one Gaius Titinius, who was also called Gadaios, to assist him in his plan. Two years before, this

---

[1]*the Palikoi:* Twin gods who were worshiped by the indigenous Sicilians. People went to their sanctuary, at a sulfurous lake near Leontini, in southeastern Sicily (Map 2), to swear sacred and binding oaths. Diodorus Siculus tells us that it also served as a refuge for fugitive slaves.

same man had been condemned to die, but he had managed to escape the imposition of the death penalty. He had been staging bandit raids, in the course of which he had murdered many free people who lived in the Sicilian countryside, but he never did any harm to slaves. This same Titinius now took with him a number of slaves who could be trusted and, on the pretense of taking sides with them in the war against the Romans, advanced on the fortified point held by the rebels. He was received as a friend. What is more, he was warmly welcomed, and because of his reputation for bravery, he was even chosen to be their commander. Titinius then betrayed the slaves' fortress to the Romans. Some of the rebels were cut down in the fighting, while others, who feared the punishment they would face if they were captured, hurled themselves off the cliff. This first revolt of fugitive slaves was, therefore, extinguished in the manner that I have just described.

After the soldiers who had taken part in this assault were released from service and had made their way to their homes, some men arrived who reported that eighty rebel slaves had cut the throat of Publius Clonius, a Roman *eques* [see glossary], and that they were now operating in large numbers. Because of the advice offered by some other men, however, the governor was dissuaded from undertaking any action against them. Since most of the soldiers had been discharged from active service, the governor's lack of decisive action provided the rebels with a much-needed opportunity to strengthen their own position. The governor did march with the soldiers he had at his disposal, but when he crossed the Alba River, he deliberately bypassed the rebels who had established themselves on the mountain named Kaprianos [Goat Mountain] and arrived at the city of Herakleia. Because the governor did not attack them, the rebels were able to spread the news of his lack of courage, and they soon incited a large number of slaves to revolt. Huge numbers of men who were well armed for battle hurried to join them. Within the next seven days, they had armed more than eight hundred men. Soon after that, they numbered no fewer than two thousand.

When the governor, Nerva, who was now at Herakleia, learned of the great increase in their numbers, he appointed Marcus Titinius as commander and assigned him six hundred soldiers from the garrison at Enna. Titinius launched an attack on the rebels, but since the slaves held the advantage both in number and because of the harsh terrain, Titinius and his men were defeated. Many of them were killed. Only by throwing away their weapons and running from the field of battle were the rest able to save themselves, and then only with difficulty. Victory in hand, the rebels were able to supply themselves with a large quantity of captured weapons and to pursue their aims with greater confidence. Now all the slaves [on the island] were encouraged by the prospect of rebellion. As more and more men turned to rebellion with every passing day, there was a sudden and unexpected increase in their number, with the result that, within a few days, they were more than six thousand.

At this point, the rebels congregated to form a popular assembly. As the first order of business presented to them, they chose a man named Salvius to be their king. He had a reputation of being skilled at foretelling the future, and he had also been a mantic[2] flute player at women's religious festivals. After he became king, Salvius ordered his subjects to avoid cities, since he considered them to be sources of laziness and excess. He divided the rebel slaves into three groups and set in command over them an equal number of officers. He ordered them to comb the countryside and to converge again at an assigned place and time. Since they were able to acquire for themselves a large number of horses and other animals by these raids, within a brief time they could equip and outfit a force of more than two thousand cavalry and no fewer than twenty thousand infantry, who were already well trained in war exercises.

Without warning, they suddenly fell on the strong city of Morgantina and subjected it to savage and unceasing assaults. With about ten thousand Italian allied troops as well as soldiers from Sicily under his command, Nerva, the governor, staged a forced march in the middle of the night to bring help to the city. Discovering that the rebels were occupied with the siege of the city, he made an attack on their fortified camp and found only a few men guarding it. He captured it quite easily. He discovered that the camp was full of women prisoners and every other sort of booty. After plundering it, he advanced on Morgantina itself. The rebels, however, suddenly turned around and attacked his forces. Since they held the higher ground, they immediately gained the upper hand in the battle. The men in the Roman governor's forces turned and ran from the field of battle. When the king of the rebels issued a proclamation that no man was to be killed who threw down his arms, most of the Roman soldiers cast away their weapons and ran for their lives. In this way, Salvius outmaneuvered his opponents and managed to take back his camp. By this complete victory over his enemies, he was able to get possession of many weapons. Because of the humane proclamation of the king, no more than six hundred Italians and Sicilians died in the battle, while more than four thousand were taken prisoner.

[2]*mantic:* prophetic.

Since many more men flocked to his side because of his successes, Salvius now had double the former force under his command and became lord of the plains region of Sicily. For this reason, Salvius made another attempt to take Morgantina by siege. He issued a proclamation in which he promised freedom to all the slaves in the city. But when their masters countered with the same offer of freedom to any slave who joined them in the fight to defend the city, the slaves chose the masters' offer. Indeed, by their zealous efforts in the battle, these slaves helped repel the siege. When the Roman governor later rescinded these grants of freedom, most of the slaves ran away and joined the rebels.

Large numbers of slaves were being incited to rebellion in the rural areas around Segesta and Lilybaeum, and also in the lands around the neighboring cities. The leader of these slaves was a man named Athenion, a Cilician by origin, and a man who was renowned for his bravery. Athenion was a domain manager for two very wealthy brothers, but he was also experienced and highly skilled in predicting the future from the stars. He first persuaded the slaves who were under his authority, about two hundred of them, to join him. He then turned to the slaves who were on neighboring farms, so that within five days he had gathered more than a thousand under his command. When he was chosen by these people to be king and had placed a diadem on his head, Athenion conducted his rule in a manner that was opposite that of all of the other rebel groups. He did not accept all slaves who went into revolt, but turned only the best of them into soldiers. He forced the others to remain at their former tasks and had each of them take care of their own household managerial tasks and work assignments. From these people, Athenion was able to provide an abundance of supplies for his soldiers. He claimed that the gods had foretold to him, by means of the stars, that he would become king of all of Sicily. It was, therefore, necessary for him to conserve the land and all the plants and animals on it, since they now belonged to him.

When he had finally assembled more than ten thousand men, Athenion dared to lay siege to the impregnable city of Lilybaeum. Not meeting with any success there, Athenion departed from the city, saying that the gods had ordered him to take this course of action. If the slaves persisted in the siege, he said, the gods had declared that they would suffer misfortune. When he was preparing to make his retreat from the city, auxiliary troops from the Mauri of North Africa, who had been dispatched to bring assistance to the people of Lilybaeum, arrived on ships. A man named Gomon commanded the Africans. He and his men made a surprise attack by night on the forces led by Athenion, who were now marching away from the city. After killing and wounding many of the rebels, Gomon returned to the city. The rebel slaves were filled with wonder at their leader's ability to prophesy the future by interpreting the stars.

A great chaos and a mountain of evils of truly epic dimensions disrupted all of Sicily, since not only slaves but also poor persons of free birth became implicated in every kind of brigandage and lawlessness. With no compunction whatsoever, they murdered anyone whom they happened to meet, whether slave or free, so that no one would survive to report their deranged behavior. The result was that the people who lived in the cities regarded their possessions within the city walls as barely still their own, while they regarded those possessions located outside the walls as lost and enslaved to the brute force of lawlessness. In addition, large numbers of people throughout all of Sicily suffered many other wrongs.

# 45

## DIODORUS SICULUS

# The Second Slave War on the Island of Sicily: Second Version

### First Century B.C.E.

*This is the version preserved in the later "excerpts" from Diodorus's history made for the Byzantine emperor Constantine Porphyrogennetos, and in some fragments preserved by Photios.*

Not only did the mass of slaves who moved to open rebellion overrun the country, but even free persons who lived in the countryside and had no possessions of their own turned to robbery and lawless behavior. Both because of their poverty and because of the general conditions of lawlessness, the poor citizens of the cities burst out into the countryside. Organized in criminal gangs, they drove off herds of cattle, carried off the crops that had been stored in granaries, and murdered anyone

Diodorus Siculus, *Library of History,* 36.11.1–3, 36.7.1–10.3 [= *Excerpts of Constantine,* 314, 390; Photios, *Library,* 389–90].

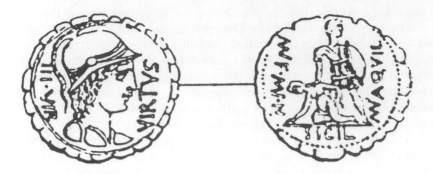

**Figure 5.** *Coin Issued ca. 70 B.C.E. Commemorating Manius Aquillius's Victory in the Second Slave War*

Roman military men who won great victories over the slaves in Sicily were remembered by their descendants who wished to profit from their ancestors' achievements. This coin was issued by Manius Aquillius, one of the three "moneyers" responsible for striking coinage for the Roman state around 70 B.C.E., immediately after the Spartacus slave war. Obviously, he wished to evoke the memory of the glorious achievements of his grandfather of the same name, who, as consul in 101 B.C.E. and proconsul in 100 B.C.E., ended the second slave war in Sicily and celebrated a minor triumph for it in 99 B.C.E. On one side of the coin is the caption "Virtvs" (courage or manliness). On the other side is the name of the moneyer—"Manius Aquillius, son of Manius, grandson of Manius"—with a picture of his ancestor standing astride and holding up the half-nude, drooping figure of a woman who is the personification of the Roman province of Sicily.

Ernest Babelon, *Description historique et chronologique des monnaies de la République romaine,* vol. 1, Paris, 1885, p. 213, no 2.

whom they happened to meet, whether free or slave, so that no one would survive to bring back a report of their madness and criminality. There was general anarchy both because there was no Roman rule to dispense justice to anyone and because many people simply usurped power, for which they were not answerable to anyone. The suffering that they caused was immense. For this reason, every place suffered from pillage. The poor had simply usurped the power to dispossess the rich of their property. Because of this wholly unexpected and unforeseen shift in fortune, the same men who previously had been among the leading men in their cities in honor and wealth were not only losing their property through acts of violence at the hands of fugitive slaves but also were being forced to endure insolent and humiliating treatment at the hands of free persons. All such men who remained in the cities, therefore, considered their property within the city gates as barely still their own, while they now considered their property located outside the city walls as belonging to others and as enslaved to the brute force of criminality. There was chaos in the cities and a complete rejection of what was right according to the laws. The rebellious slaves had power over the open countryside and made the rural lands impassable, since they harbored deep and long-remembered hatreds for their masters and were never satisfied with whatever good fortune came their way. What is more, the minds of the slaves who were still in the cities were becoming infected with the disease of rebellion. As they moved ever closer to open revolt, they became objects of great fear to their masters.

Following the siege of Morgantina, Salvius conducted raids over the countryside as far as the plain of Leontini. He gathered together his whole army, having conscripted no less than thirty thousand men. He made sacrifices to the Palikian heroes and made them an offering of one sea-dyed purple cloak[1] in gratitude for his victory. He then announced that he was King Tryphon[2] and was hailed as a king by the rebel slaves. Intending to seize Triokala [Triocala] and to construct a palace for himself at that place, he sent a dispatch to Athenion, summoning the man just like a king would summon one of his generals. Everyone assumed that Athenion would contest primacy with Tryphon and that with the conflict between them, the slave war would easily be brought to an end. But Fortune, as if satisfied to increase the power of the fugitive slaves, caused the leaders to come to an agreement. Tryphon immediately went to Triokala with his military force. Athenion also came with three thousand men and subordinated himself as military commander to Tryphon, the king. He had sent the rest of his force to overrun the countryside and incite the slaves to rebellion. Later, Tryphon suspected that Athenion might attack him if given the opportunity, so he ordered Athenion to be placed in detention.

Tryphon furnished the strong and rugged fortress at Triokala with lavish adornments and made it even more impregnable than it had been. The place was called Triokala because it has three excellent advantages. First, it has flowing spring waters, which are exceptional for their sweetness. Second, the surrounding countryside is richly planted in vines

---

[1]*sea-dyed purple cloak:* purple was the color of royalty, "sea-dyed" because the purple dye secreted by murex molluscs was used.

[2]*King Tryphon:* a violent, freebooting entrepreneur of violence from Cilicia named Tryphon, who claimed to be the legitimate king of Syria, had held sway over parts of the eastern Mediterranean in the late 140s and early 130s B.C.E.

and olive trees and is wonderfully suited to agriculture. Third, the place itself is situated on top of a huge and impregnable rock and is of forbidding appearance. Tryphon constructed a defensive wall, eight stades[3] in circumference, around the city, excavated a deep ditch around it, and began to use the place as his royal quarters. Tryphon filled Triokala with an abundance of all the supplies that are needed to live the good life. He also constructed a royal palace and a marketplace capable of serving a very large number of people. From men who were exceptional in their intelligence, he selected a sufficient number whom he appointed to be his formal advisers and counselors. Whenever King Tryphon conducted official business, he donned a purple Roman toga and a wide-bordered Greek cloak. He also had lictors holding the symbolic axes[4] to precede him, as well as all of the other accoutrements that are suitable to the embellishment of royal power.

To confront the rebels, the Roman Senate appointed Lucius Licinius Lucullus. He had 14,000 Italian and Roman soldiers; 800 Bithynians, Thessalians, and Akarnanians; 600 Lucanians, commanded by [Tiberius] Cleptius, a military man who was renowned for his bravery; and 600 other men, making a grand total of 17,000.[5] He held Sicily with these forces.

At this point, Tryphon, who was beginning to plan the war against the Romans, removed the legal charges against Athenion and released him from confinement. Tryphon's preference was to prepare for the confrontation with the Romans at Triokala, but Athenion advised that the slaves should not trap themselves by accepting a siege but rather that they should fight in open terrain. The latter plan won the day, and the army, no fewer than forty thousand strong, was established in camps close to Skirthaia. The Roman camp was twelve stades[6] away from theirs. At first, there were just a few sharp skirmishes between the two armies, but then both sides set out their lines, and the battle was joined there and then. Many men were killed on both sides. Athenion, who had two hundred cavalrymen fighting with him, killed everyone in his path, filling the area around him with enemy corpses. But when he was wounded in both knees, and then took a third wound, he was no longer

---

[3]*eight stades:* a little under one mile.

[4]*symbolic axes:* A Roman magistrate was preceded by men holding bundles of wooden rods (*fasces*) with axes embedded in them that symbolized the power of the magistrate to discipline by the use of physical force.

[5]This is the total given in the manuscript, although the figures add up to only 16,000. Tiberius Cleptius (or Clepitius) would become an important war leader of the Lucanians in the armed struggle that the Italian allies waged against Rome in 90–88 B.C.E.

[6]*twelve stades:* about 1.4 miles.

able to fight. The fugitive slaves began to lose their morale. Finally, they turned and ran from the field of battle. Athenion was thought to be dead and so escaped notice. By pretending to be dead, he made his escape during the night and so saved his own life.

The Romans won a brilliant victory. Tryphon and his supporters ran from the field of battle. In their attempt to escape, many men were cut down. In total, no fewer than twenty thousand of the rebels were killed. Those who survived made their way under cover of darkness to Triokala. If the Roman general had followed them in hot pursuit, it would have been easy to kill them all. The general body of the slaves was so downcast and depressed that some of them even urged that they should return to their masters and submit themselves again voluntarily to their masters' authority. But the opposite opinion—that they should fight to the death and should not surrender to their enemies—won the day.

On the ninth day after the battle [at Skirthaia], the Roman general arrived at Triokala to place it under siege. After inflicting some casualties and suffering some himself, the general withdrew, defeated. The rebels regained their confidence. Whether because of simple laziness or because of some gifts [bribes] that had been given to him, the Roman commander did not accomplish what had to be done. For this reason, he was later summoned before a court and punished by the Romans.

Gaius Servilius, who was sent out as praetor in succession to Lucullus, accomplished nothing worthy of memory. For this inactivity, Servilius, like Lucullus, was later condemned to exile by a Roman court. When Tryphon died, Athenion became the successor to his rule. He placed cities under siege, overran the countryside with impunity, and became the lord of many men, while Servilius did nothing to prevent him.

It was at the end of the year when Gaius Marius was elected consul at Rome for the fifth time and Gaius[7] Aquillius for the first time. Aquillius was dispatched to repress the rebels, and because of his personal bravery, he crushed them in a brilliantly conducted battle. He fought a hand-to-hand duel with Athenion, the king of the rebels, and beat him in a heroic contest (see Figure 6). Aquillius killed Athenion, but in the process he sustained a severe head wound. Later, when he recovered from the wound following medical treatment, Aquillius continued to campaign against the remnant of the rebels, who now numbered about ten thousand. When they were not able to hold out against his attacks and they retreated to rugged defensive positions, Aquillius left no avenue untried until he finally defeated the besieged rebels.

[7]Diodorus is incorrect. His first name was Manius.

Even after this defeat, there were a thousand rebels who survived with Satyros as their general. At first, Aquillius thought that he would attempt to defeat them with the brute force of arms. Later, however, by using negotiators, he obtained their surrender. He exempted the slave prisoners from summary punishment and instead took them to Rome, where he intended to have them fight as gladiators in combat with wild beasts. Some people say that they brought their lives to a most glorious end when they refused to do battle with the wild animals and instead cut each other down in front of the public altars. Satyros himself killed the last man. Then Satyros took his life with his own hand, dying like a hero. Thus, the war of the slaves in Sicily, a war that had lasted nearly four years, reached its tragic finale.

All of the documents that follow are minor sources for the history of the second slave war on Sicily.

## 46

## ATHENAEUS

# The Second Slave War on the Island of Sicily and the Contemporary Slave Rebellion at Athens

### Second Century C.E.

---

*Athenaeus, a compiler of varied types of information, refers to earlier writers on the second slave war on Sicily, including the Jewish historian Caecilius from Kalê Aktê.*

---

Larensis said, "But every Roman, as you well know, my good Masurius, owns a very large number of slaves. In fact, there are many who own a myriad,[1] double that number or even more. They do not own them to produce profits, as in the case of Nicias, the very wealthy Athenian.

---

[1]If the Greek word *myrias* (myriad) is to be taken literally, which it probably is not, it would mean "ten thousand."

Athenaeus, *Deipnosophistae,* 6.272.d–f.

Rather, the majority of Romans employ the largest number of their slaves to accompany them as a way of displaying their prestige. Most of the slaves at Athens, on the other hand, who were numbered in myriads, worked in shackles in the mines. At any rate, Posidonius the philosopher, whose words you have repeatedly brought to our attention, states that they rebelled, murdered the men who guarded the mines, captured the acropolis of Sounion, and plundered Attica for a long time. This was at the same time that the second uprising of the slaves on Sicily took place. There were many of these slave rebellions, and more than a million slaves [literally, 'hundreds of myriads'] were killed. A history of the slave wars was written by Caecilius, the rhetor from Kale Akte in Sicily."

# 47

## CASSIUS DIO

# The Actions of the Roman Governor of Sicily, Publius Licinius Nerva, in 104 B.C.E.

### Third Century C.E.

*In his history of Rome written at the beginning of the third century C.E., Dio Cassius records actions taken by the Roman governor of Sicily.*

When he was governor of the island of Sicily, Publius Licinius Nerva circulated a notice that any slaves who had charges to bring against their masters could come to him and he would help them. Nerva did this either because he had learned that some slaves were not being fairly treated in certain respects or because he was seeking personal gain, for he was the type of man who was not immune to bribery. Under the terms of his proclamation, many slaves began to congregate. Some of them declared that they were being treated unfairly, and others specified grievances against their masters, since they believed that they were being given an opportunity to right the wrongs that had been done to

Cassius Dio, *Histories*, 27, fragment 101 [93.1–3].

them, but without recourse to bloodshed. The freeborn slave owners, however, after taking counsel among themselves, refused to concede any of the slaves' demands. Because of the pressures being brought on him by both sides, Nerva became nervous and feared that great harm would be done by the side that came off the worse in this confrontation. He therefore refused to hear any more of the slaves' petitions. Instead, he sent them away, believing that they would not suffer any harm [on returning to their masters] or, at least, that since they were dispersed, they would be less likely to cause more trouble. The slaves, however, who were afraid of their masters because they had dared raise their voices against them, gathered together in a group and, by agreement among themselves, turned to banditry.

# 48

## FLORUS

## *Athenion as Leader of the Second Slave War*

### Second Century *C.E.*

*For the first half of this section, Florus's account of the first slave war in Sicily, see Document 40.*

The island of Sicily had barely recovered [from the ravages of the first slave war] when, in the governorship of Servilius, the command [of the fugitive slaves] passed from the hands of the Syrian into those of the Cilician. He was a herdsman named Athenion, who had murdered his master, freed the man's slaves from their barracks, and formed them into regular army units. Athenion arrayed himself in a purple robe, carried a silver scepter, and crowned himself like a king. He raised an army that was just as large as that of his demented predecessor, but he conducted his operations with even greater savagery, as if he were seeking vengeance for Eunus. Athenion plundered villages, towns, and fortresses. He vented his rage on loyal slaves in these communities with even greater violence than he did on their masters, since he considered the slaves to be traitors.

Florus, "The Slave War," in *A Synopsis of Roman History,* 2.7.9–12.

He also routed the armies commanded by Roman praetors and captured the army camps of Servilius and Lucullus. But Titus Aquilius[1] followed the good example set by Perperna. He reduced the enemy to extreme conditions by cutting off their supplies and then easily destroyed their forces in battle once they had been severely weakened by starvation. The slaves would have surrendered, but because of their fear of the punishments that we would inflict on them, they preferred to commit suicide. It was not possible to exact the death penalty even from their leader, although he fell into our hands alive. After he was captured, the mobs around him began to argue over his arrest, and the disputants tore his body to pieces like so much plunder.

## 49

### CASSIUS DIO

## *Athenion's Attack on the City of Messana*
### *Third Century C.E.*

*In his general history of Rome, Cassius Dio reports the attack by the slaves on the city of Messana in Sicily.*

The people of Messana, who had not expected to meet with any harm, had deposited all of their most valuable and precious possessions in the place for safekeeping. When he learned of this, Athenion, the Cilician who held command over the bandits, attacked the Messanians when they were holding a public festival in the suburbs. He killed many of them as they ran for safety and almost succeeded in capturing the city itself. . . . After building a wall to fortify Makella, a strong point, Athenion proceeded violently to pillage the surrounding countryside.

---

[1]Florus is incorrect. It should be Manius Aquillius.

---

Cassius Dio, *Histories,* fragment 104 [93.4].

# 50

## CICERO

# Athenion as a Model of Evil Power

### First Century B.C.E.

*In a later court speech, the senator Cicero recollects the role of the slave leader Athenion in the slave war on Sicily.*

You must know, therefore, that for these three years it was not Athenion, who never captured a single town, but rather the fugitive Timarchides [one of the Roman governor Verres' freedmen] who was the real king of all the towns in Sicily. . . . Is not Verres' entire treatment of Sicily of such a kind that even if Athenion himself, the king of the fugitive slaves, had won the war, he would not have acted this way?

Cicero, *Against Verres*, 2.2.136, 2.3.66.

# 51

## CICERO

# The Destruction of Sicily Caused by the Slaves

### First Century B.C.E.

*In a later court speech, the senator Cicero remembers the destruction done by the slaves in the second slave war on the island of Sicily.*

In the days when Sicily was tormented by the wars that Rome fought against Carthage, and on two later occasions, within the memory of our fathers and ourselves, when huge forces of fugitive slaves overran the province, there still was no irreparable damage done to the peasant farmers . . . and the praetors who were successors to . . . Publius Rupilius and

Cicero, *Against Verres*, 2.3.125.

Manius Aquillius in this province didn't have to scrape together what was left of the farmers. Didn't Verres, along with his helper Apronius, bring greater calamities upon the province of Sicily than Hasdrubal, with his Carthaginian army, or Athenion, with his great force of fugitive slaves?

## 52

### CICERO

## Aquillius Is Compelled to Dispense Aid to Sicilian Cities

### First Century B.C.E.

*In the following passage, Cicero points out that Sicily, which normally shipped surplus grain to Rome, now has to depend on Roman aid.*

And during the war with the fugitive slaves, Manius Aquillius even had to make loans of cereal grain to the cities of Sicily.

Cicero, *On the Agrarian Law,* 2.83.

## 53

### CICERO

## The Romans Reward Aquillius for Ending the Slave War

### First Century B.C.E.

*In a later court speech, the senator Cicero calls to mind the way in which the victorious Roman commander in the Sicilian slave war was lauded.*

Cicero, *In Defense of Flaccus,* 39.98.

Our forefathers, who had convicted Manius Aquillius based on the evidence of many witnesses on a variety of extortion charges, absolved him from the judgment of the court because he had waged war so bravely against the fugitive slaves.

## 54

### CICERO

# Roman Governors of Sicily Take Measures to Prevent the Recurrence of Slave Uprisings

### First Century B.C.E.

*In a later court speech, Cicero mentions repressive measures taken by Roman governors of Sicily.*

And as for the infectious disease of the slave war, why should this be preached about by you [Verres], any more than by all the other men who were assigned provinces to govern? Is it because there were wars against fugitive slaves in Sicily at some earlier time? But it is for this very reason that the province is, and has been, in the least danger. For ever since the time when Manius Aquillius ended his governorship of the province, the measures taken and the decrees issued by all governors have been consistent: that no slave is to possess a weapon.

I'll tell you an old story—one probably already well known to all of you because of its exemplary harshness. When Lucius Domitius was governor of Sicily, an enormous wild boar was brought to him. Admiring it, Domitius asked who had killed it. When he heard that it was a herder who was owned by a certain man, he ordered the herdsman to be summoned before him. Expecting praise and perhaps even a reward, the herdsman eagerly hurried to the governor. Domitius asked who had killed such a huge wild animal. The man replied, "I did—with a hunting spear." Whereupon the man was immediately crucified by order of the governor. Perhaps this seems harsh. I won't argue either

Cicero, *Against Verres*, 2.5.7; 2.5.8.

side of the issue, but I will say this: Domitius preferred cruelty in punishment rather than to seem lax by overlooking a crime. . . .

When these measures had been enforced in the province, at a time when Italy was ablaze with the war against our allies, Gaius Norbanus,[1] who was not the keenest or the bravest of men, was left in perfect peace. For Sicily was already guarding itself so well that it was not possible that any war could arise in it. This was the case, especially since no people are as closely linked to the Sicilians by common interests as are our businessmen, because of their day-to-day dealings, material interests, plans, and sentiments. And the affairs of the Sicilians themselves are so well organized that peace is something that is very useful to them. Indeed, they so cherish the rule of the Roman people that they have no desire at all that our government should be diminished or radically changed. The measures taken by our governors and the discipline enforced by the slave masters safeguard them against the dangers of another slave war. Therefore, no internal troubles could possibly arise from the province itself.

**Figure 6.** *Coin Issued in 18 B.C.E. Commemorating Manius Aquillius's Victory in the Second Slave War*

The long memory of military success continues. Here we have another coin issued by an even more distant descendant of Manius Aquillius, the moneyer Lucius Aquillius Florus, in 18 B.C.E., perhaps six or more generations removed from his ancestor. The first Roman emperor, Caesar Augustus, is portrayed on one side of the coin. On the other is the same motif (Figure 5) of Manius Aquillius supporting "Sicily" after saving her from the ravages of the second slave war. Lucius Aquillius Florus had been caught on the wrong side in the civil wars of the 30s B.C.E. and needed to reestablish his political credentials. By issuing this coin in 18 B.C.E., he hoped to reaffirm his loyalty to the state.

---

[1]*Gaius Norbanus:* Roman governor of Sicily, probably in 90–88 B.C.E.

# 55

# Slingshot Ammunition Used by the Slaves and Greek Allies of the Romans
## ca. 104–100 B.C.E.

*A large number of slingshot bullets have been discovered in Roman Sicily, in the western part of the island around Panormus, in the eastern part of the island south of the plain of Leontini, and around Enna itself (Document 42). Some of the ammunition is inscribed with the name of a deity or a leader under whom victory was expected. The examples included here seem to have been used by the slave forces led by Athenion and Salvius (a.k.a. King Tryphon), who appear to be named on some of them. Note that any close identification with religious forces and specific deities is absent from the Latin inscriptions on slingshot bullets used by Roman forces.*

*The following slingshot bullets were found in the Sciacca region of western Sicily, about fifteen miles west of Agrigento, on the south coast.*

| | |
|---|---|
| 2407.3 | Victory (under) Zeus Keraunos [Zeus the Thunderer] [decorated with a lightning bolt] |
| [Unedited] | Victory (under) Athênion [decorated with a lightning bolt on the same side and with a picture of a scorpion on the other] |

*These slingshot bullets were found predominantly in the southeastern corner of Sicily, in the region between Palazzolo Acreide and Noto.*

| | |
|---|---|
| 2407.1 | Victory (under) Athena |
| 2407.2 | Victory (under) Artemis |
| 2407.5 | Victory (under) Heraklês |
| 2497.6 | Victory (under) Korê |
| 2407.7 | Victory (under) the Mother [or] the Mothers[1] |

[1] *the Mother/Mothers:* the "Mother" goddess, or the "Mothers," also identified with Ceres and her daughter Persephone.

*Inscriptiones Graecae,* vol. 14, 608–10, no. 2407; Giacomo Manganaro, "Monete e ghiande inscritte degli schiavi ribelli in Sicilia," *Chiron* 12 (1982): 238–44 and plates 6–8; C. Zangemeister, *Glandes Plumbeae Latine Inscriptae [= Ephemeris Epigraphica]* (Berlin, 1885), x–xviii.

| 2407.8 | Victory (under) Athenion [decorated with a lightning bolt] |
| [Unedited] | Victory (under) Sôs [Salvius?] |
| [Unedited] | Victory (under) Tryphôn |

*Other slingshot bullets that had Greek written on them were inscribed with the formal civic identifications of citizens of Greek city-states in Italy. These bullets seem to be ammunition used by Greeks fighting for the Romans against the slaves. Not only are these bullets more stereotypical and formal than those used by the slaves, but they also are decorated with different emblems. The "tribes" and "phratries" (brotherhoods) reflect the units of the citizen body into which adult males were divided not just for political purposes, such as voting in elections, but also for military service.*

| 2407.10 | First Tribe. Phratria Eng. Nikias son of Politas [Catana: man on bended knee, a helmet to the left and a shield on the right] |
| 2407.11 | Second Tribe. Phratria Altri. Philonas son of Eupolemos [Catana: same decoration as on previous one] |
| 2407.12 | Third Tribe. Phratria Katêl. [name lost] son of Stratôn [Troina, a Greek city-state to the northeast of Enna: symbols of Herakles] |
| 2407.13 | Second Tribe. Phratria Lakyn. Agelaos son of Pyrrhia [near Bronte, about thirty miles northeast of Enna] |
| 2407.14 | Second Tribe. Phratria Ple. Phintylos son of Pheidios [Assorus, about twelve miles east northeast of Enna] |

# 7

# The Spartacus Slave War, 73–71 B.C.E.

Between 73 and 71 B.C.E., large areas of the Italian peninsula south of Rome were thrown into a state of upheaval by the sudden outbreak of the third great slave war. This war was sparked by an incident involving the escape of a group of slave gladiators from their training school at Capua, the city that was the de facto capital of the wealthy region of Campania. A gladiator named Spartacus led the rebel slaves. Although their initial forays were limited to the region around Mount Vesuvius and the Bay of Naples, the revolt seems to have rapidly acquired a large number of adherents. The initial Roman response was slow and involved only what were in effect police or national guard units dispatched from Rome or recruited locally in emergency drafts. After the defeat of several of these forces, the Roman Senate and people began to take the rebellion more seriously and to assign high-level military commands to deal with the uprising.

The war lasted for two years and ended only after legionary armies were placed under the command of Marcus Licinius Crassus. These forces, which had full battle capability and the training needed to deploy elaborate siege and containment works, were finally able to defeat the slaves and to kill their leader, Spartacus. Pompey the Great mopped up some dispersed and isolated groups of rebel slaves after the final battle. Reverberations of the war, however, continued for a decade after the final defeat of Spartacus. Small guerrilla-like bands of peasants and slaves were still being repressed by Roman forces in southern Italy in the late 60s B.C.E.

# 56

## PLUTARCH

# The Spartacus Slave War

### Second Century C.E.

*Plutarch is most famous for his* Parallel Lives, *or the long series of biographies in which he compares the lives of some famous Greeks and Romans. Here he compares the Roman general Marcus Licinius Crassus with the fifth-century* B.C.E. *Athenian general Nicias. Plutarch is one of the most important sources for the Spartacus slave war, though not for Spartacus himself As a slave, gladiator, and rebel, Spartacus would not have met Plutarch's criteria for a model citizen. Instead, we get a glimpse of the slave leader in Plutarch's portrait of Marcus Licinius Crassus, the Roman commander of the legions in Italy during the last year of the war.*

The revolt of the gladiators and the destruction of Italy that most people call the Spartacus war had its origin in the following cause. At Capua a man named Lentulus Batiatus was a trainer and entrepreneur of gladiators, most of whom were Gauls and Thracians. These men were compelled to engage in gladiatorial combats, not for any crimes they had committed but because of the unjust behavior of their owners. Two hundred of them planned to make an escape, but information concerning their plan was betrayed. Those who were forewarned that their plan had been divulged still persisted in their attempt. Seventy-two of them made good their escape, grabbing kitchen knives and cooking skewers on their way out [of the gladiatorial school]. On the road outside the school, these men happened to encounter some wagons that were loaded with weapons destined for gladiators in another city. They seized the weapons and armed themselves with them. Then, after they had taken possession of a strong point, they chose three leaders. The most important of these was Spartacus.

Spartacus was a Thracian, born among a pastoral nomadic people.[1] He not only possessed great spirit and bodily strength, but he was more

[1]Konrat Ziegler, editor of one of the standard modern texts, has argued that the original Greek text should read *tou Maidikou genous* (rather than *tou nomadikou genous,* as

Plutarch, *Life of Crassus,* 8–11.

intelligent and nobler than his fate, and he was more Greek than his [Thracian] background might indicate. People tell the following story about him when he was brought to Rome to be sold as a slave. While he was sleeping, a snake coiled up around his head. Spartacus's wife, a woman who came from the same tribe as Spartacus, was a prophetess who was possessed by ecstatic frenzies that were part of the worship of the god Dionysus. She declared that this was the sign of a tremendous and fearsome power that would bring him to an unfortunate end.[2] She was living with him at the time and ran away with him when he escaped.

In their first actions, the gladiators drove off those who were coming out of the city of Capua and seized from them many weapons that were more suitable for warfare. They happily made the exchange, throwing away their gladiatorial armaments, which they viewed as dishonorable and barbaric. Next, a Roman commander, the praetor Clodius [Gaius Claudius Glaber], was sent from Rome with three thousand soldiers. He laid siege to the gladiators on the mountain they now occupied. Clodius placed a guard post on the one narrow and difficult access road that led up the mountain. All the other parts of the mountain were formed of smooth and steep precipices, and the top of it was heavily overgrown with wild vines. The slaves cut off the useful parts of these climbing plants and wove ladders out of them. These were strong and long enough so that when they were fastened at the top of the cliffs, they reached down as far as the level plain at the foot of the mountain. All the men, except one of them, descended safely by these devices. This one man stayed behind with the weapons. When the others had reached the bottom, he dropped the arms down. Only when all of them had been thrown down did he save himself, last of all. The Romans were wholly unaware of these developments. Consequently, the slaves were able to surround them and to shock the Romans with a surprise attack. When the Romans fled, the slaves seized their camp. At this point, many of the herdsmen and shepherds from the surrounding regions—hard-bodied and swift-footed men—came to join the slaves. The slaves armed some of these men; they used others as scouts and light-armed troops.

Next, the praetor Publius Varinius was sent out in command of the Roman forces against the slaves. His subordinate officer, a man named Furius, who had two thousand men with him, engaged the slaves and

---

translated here), a reference to the specific ethnic origin of Spartacus: that he was "from the [Thracian] people called the Maidi."

[2]The manuscripts are unclear: *eutyches* can be read instead of *atyches* (which is translated here), in which case the translation would have precisely the opposite sense: "a tremendous and fearsome power that would bring him good fortune."

was defeated by them. Spartacus closely followed Varinius's adjutant and co-commander [Lucius] Cossinius, who had also been dispatched with a large force, and observed his movements. Spartacus came within a hair's breadth of capturing Cossinius at Salinae when the Roman commander was bathing. Indeed, it was with great difficulty that Cossinius managed to escape. Spartacus immediately seized his supplies and began harrying him closely. With hard pursuit and much slaughter, Spartacus captured the Roman general's camp. Cossinius himself died in the encounter. But it was by defeating the praetor Varinius in many other battles and, finally, by capturing his lictors and even the Roman commander's own horse, that Spartacus became a figure of fame and fear. Even so, he carefully considered the most probable course of events. Thinking it unlikely that he would be able to defeat the Roman forces, Spartacus instead led his army toward the Alps. Once they crossed the mountains, he thought that it would be the best, indeed the necessary, course of action for the men to disperse to their own homelands, some to Thrace and others to Gaul. But his men, who now had confidence in their great number and had grander ideas in their heads, did not obey him. Rather, they began to pillage Italy far and wide.

At this point, it was no longer the unworthiness and shame of the slave rebellion that so vexed the Senate. Rather, it was because of fear and the danger of the situation that they dispatched both consuls together to the war, much as they would send consuls to a regular war of the greatest difficulty and magnitude. Of the two commanders, [Lucius] Gellius [Publicola] made a sudden surprise attack on a force of Germans who, because of their insolent arrogance, had separated themselves from Spartacus's main forces. He slaughtered the whole lot of them. But when [Gnaeus Cornelius] Lentulus, the other consul, surrounded Spartacus with his large battlefield forces, Spartacus suddenly rushed at them and engaged them in battle. He defeated Lentulus's legates and captured all of their supplies. Just as Spartacus was driving toward the Alps, however, [Gaius] Cassius [Longinus], the governor of Cisalpine Gaul, who had many thousands of soldiers[3] under his command, blocked his way. In the battle that took place, Cassius was defeated, with the loss of many men. Indeed, he made his own escape only with difficulty.

When the Senate learned of these events, it angrily ordered the consuls to cease operations and chose Crassus as the general to be put in charge of the war. Many Roman noblemen joined Crassus in the conduct of the war, both because of his great reputation and because

---

[3]Literally, "a myriad," or exactly ten thousand.

of their personal friendship with him. To receive the brunt of Spartacus's attack, Crassus stationed his forces on the borders of Picenum.[4] In the meantime, he sent his legate Mummius with two legions on a long, roundabout route to encircle Spartacus from the rear. He ordered Mummius to follow the enemy closely, but not to join battle with them or even to skirmish with them. When the first good opportunity presented itself, however, Mummius eagerly rushed into battle and was defeated. Many of his men were killed, and many others dropped their weapons and ran from the field of battle to save themselves. Later, when Crassus received Mummius, he gave him a rough going-over. And when he rearmed Mummius's soldiers, Crassus demanded formal promises from them that they would not "lose" their weapons. What is more, Crassus selected five hundred of the soldiers who had been the first to run from the field of battle, especially those who had displayed open cowardice, and divided them into fifty groups of ten each. He then executed one man who had been selected by lot from each group. He thereby revived an ancestral punishment of soldiers that had not been used for a long time. It is a shameful type of death in its mode of execution: Many terrible things are done during the imposition of the penalty, while all the other soldiers are forced to look on as spectators.

After he had punished the men in this way, Crassus led them against the enemy. But Spartacus went up through the hinterland of Lucania toward the sea. When he came to the Strait [of Messana], he happened to meet with some Cilician pirates and so decided that he would try to seize Sicily. Spartacus hoped that by landing two thousand men on the island, he would rekindle the fires of the slave war there, a conflagration that had been put out only a short time before and needed just a little more fuel to burst into flames again. Although the Cilicians made an agreement with Spartacus and accepted his gifts, they deceived him and sailed away. So once again Spartacus marched inland away from the sea and quartered his army on the peninsula of Rhegium. When Crassus moved up with his forces and saw the course of action that was suggested by the natural lay of the terrain, he decided to build a wall across the peninsula. At the same time, this enterprise would keep his soldiers from sloth and supplies from the enemy.

The project was an immense one. Contrary to all expectations, Crassus finished it and brought it to completion within a brief time. He ran a ditch from sea to sea, across the narrow neck of land, for a length of three hundred stades.[5] In width and in depth, the defensive ditch had

[4]Probably a mistake. Instead, Plutarch probably meant the region around Picentia, south of Rome.

[5]*three hundred stades:* about thirty-five miles.

the same measurement of fifteen feet. Above the ditch, he constructed a wall that was astonishing in its height and strength. At first, Spartacus showed no concern for the project, and even showed contempt for it. But when his supplies began to run out and he wished to move off the peninsula, he recognized the impediment formed by the wall and realized that he could receive nothing unless it was from within the peninsula itself. So, on a windy and snowy night in winter, he had a small part of the trench filled in with earth, wood, and tree branches and thus was able to get a third of his army across.

Crassus was now afraid that a sudden impulse would strike Spartacus to make a march on Rome. But he took heart when he saw that, because of a difference of opinion, some of Spartacus's men had separated from his main force and had made a camp by themselves alongside a lake in Lucania. There are stories about this lake, whose waters, they say, turn sweet for a time and then return to being bitter and undrinkable. Crassus attacked these men and drove them away from the lake, but he was not able to complete their slaughter or to engage in a hot pursuit of their remnants because of the sudden appearance of Spartacus, who put a stop to their flight.

Crassus had written earlier to the Senate that it was necessary to summon [Lucius Licinius] Lucullus from Thrace and Pompey from Spain. But now he changed his mind and was in a hurry to bring the war to a conclusion before these men arrived, knowing full well that the reputation of success would belong to the one who came last and who brought help to end the war, not to himself. He therefore decided to make an attack on the slaves, first on those led by Gaius Gannicus and Castus, who had separated from Spartacus and were making their own army camps. He dispatched 6,000 men to occupy a high ridge of land and ordered them to try to hide themselves. The men did their best to elude discovery by covering their helmets, but two women who were making ritual sacrifices on behalf of the enemy spotted them. They would have found themselves in serious danger had not Crassus quickly appeared and engaged the slaves in a fight that was to be the hardest of all the battles he ever fought. He killed 12,300 of the enemy in the battle. He later discovered that only two of them had wounds in their backs. All the others had stood their ground in the line of battle and had died fighting the Romans.

After he had been defeated in this battle, Spartacus made his way upland into the mountains of Petelia. He was pursued by [Lucius] Quintus [also Quintius or Quinctius] one of the officers serving under Crassus, and by the quaestor [Gnaeus Tremelius] Scrofa. When Spartacus suddenly turned on them, there was panic among the Roman soldiers, who turned and ran from the field of battle. Somehow they were able to drag the quaestor, who had been wounded, from danger and save his life. This success destroyed Spartacus's army. It was the point at which a band of mere fugitive slaves came to think too highly of themselves. They no longer considered it honorable to engage in tactics that required perpetual retreat and flight. Consequently, the men no longer obeyed their leaders.

As soon as they were back on the road and in full armament, they confronted their officers and forced them to lead the army back again through Lucania against the Romans—the very thing Crassus wanted them to do. For the advance of Pompey and his army had already been reported, and there were some people (indeed, not a few of them) who were beginning to assign the victory to him. Crassus, therefore, advanced quickly to force a battle in order to bring the war to an end. He labored hard for this purpose, and after establishing his camps close to the enemy, he began to dig a defensive trench. The slaves jumped into this trench and began to fight with the men who were digging it. Then, as more and more men from either side jumped into the fray to help their fellow soldiers, Spartacus recognized that his hand was being forced and arranged his whole army in battle formation. When his horse was brought to him, Spartacus drew his sword and shouted that if he won the battle, he would have many fine horses that belonged to the enemy, but if he lost, he would have no need of a horse. With that, he killed the animal. Then, driving through weapons and the wounded, Spartacus rushed at Crassus. He never reached the Roman, although he killed two centurions, who fell with him. In the end, when all of those around him had abandoned him, Spartacus stood alone. Surrounded by a great many of the enemy, he was cut down while defending himself.

Although Crassus had experienced good fortune, had displayed the best skills of a field commander, and had exposed himself to great physical danger, the fame of this success ultimately escaped him and fell instead to Pompey. The reason was that the five thousand slaves who were fleeing from the field of the battle ran into Pompey's oncoming forces and were slaughtered. In consequence, Pompey was able to write a formal report to the Senate that although Crassus had conquered the fugitive slaves in the open, he [Pompey] had extinguished the war to its very roots. So it was Pompey who celebrated a marvelous triumph for his [earlier] victories over Sertorius in Spain [in 73 B.C.E.]. Crassus, on the other hand, did not even attempt to ask for a great triumph for himself. Indeed, it seemed ignoble for him to celebrate even the lesser triumph . . . that the Romans call an *ovatio* for a war fought against slaves.

# 57

## PLUTARCH

# Pompey the Great's Involvement in the Repression of Spartacus

### Second Century C.E.

Plutarch recounts the events of Pompey's life after he defeated the Roman rebel Sertorius in Spain in 73 B.C.E.

After these events, Pompey remained in Spain for as long as it was necessary to settle the great troubles there and to bring an end to the embers [of rebellion] that were still smoldering in that place. He then brought his army back to Italy, where he learned that the slave war had just reached its height. For this very reason, the commander in the war, Crassus, hurried, perhaps even at considerable risk, to force a confrontation with the enemy. He met with great success, killing 12,300 of the enemy. But even with this favorable result, fate somehow managed to throw success Pompey's way, since 5,000 of the slaves who were fleeing from the battle ran into his oncoming forces. He killed all of them. Pompey then wrote to the Senate that although Crassus had defeated the gladiators in a battle, he [Pompey] had extinguished the war to its very roots.

Plutarch, *Life of Pompey,* 21.1–4.

# 58

## PLUTARCH

# Marcus Crassus and the Final Defeat of Spartacus

### Second Century C.E.

The Greek biographer Plutarch mentions the role of the Roman military commander Marcus Crassus in the final defeat of Spartacus.

Plutarch, *Comparison of Nicias and Crassus,* 3.2.

As for myself, I cannot praise Crassus for pressing forward in his actions against Spartacus more quickly than safety would dictate, even if, in his desire to acquire honor, he was afraid that Pompey, who had just arrived with his forces, would steal his fame, just as Mummius stole the glory for the capture of the city of Corinth from Metellus.

# 59

## PLUTARCH

# Cato the Younger in the Spartacus War

### Second Century C.E.

*Plutarch is reporting on the virtues displayed by Marcus Porcius Cato the Younger (later called Uticensis) during the war against Spartacus. He compares his achievements with those of his glorious ancestor, his great-grandfather Cato the Elder, author of the treatise on managing slave farms (Document 2).*

When the slave war that they called the Spartacus war broke out, in which [Lucius] Gellius [Publicola] was the Roman commander, Cato wanted to share in the combat because of his brother [Caepio, a tribune in the army]. Cato did not have as much opportunity to display his eagerness for combat or to exercise his virtues as he wished, since the war was not one that was well commanded. Despite the effeminacy and laxity of those who fought in the war, however, Cato was able to display the virtues of order, self-control, and courage in every situation that he faced, and he showed that he was in no respect less a man than the elder Cato.

Plutarch, *Life of Cato the Younger*, 8.1–2.

# 60

## APPIAN

# The Spartacus Slave War
### Second Century C.E.

*The second-century Greek historian Appian begins his account by recount-
ing the events of 73 B.C.E., following Pompey's defeat of Sertorius in Spain
and his return to Italy.*

At about this same time, at the city of Capua in Italy, gladiators were
being trained to fight in spectacles. Spartacus, a Thracian whom the
Romans had imprisoned and then sold to be trained as a gladiator, had
once fought as a soldier for the Roman army. He persuaded about seventy of the enslaved men to risk a break for freedom rather than to
allow themselves to be put on display for the entertainment of others.
Using force to overcome their guards, the men made their escape. The
fugitives armed themselves with wooden clubs and daggers that they
seized from travelers on the roads nearby, and then rushed to take refuge on mount Vesuvius. Many fugitive slaves and even some free men
from the surrounding countryside came to this place to join Spartacus.
They began to stage bandit raids on nearby settlements. Spartacus had
his fellow gladiators Oenomaus and Crixus as his two subordinate commanders. Since Spartacus divided the profits of his raiding into equal
shares, he soon attracted a very large number of followers.

The first man the Romans sent out against Spartacus was Varinius
Glaber, and then, after him, they dispatched Publius Valerius.[1] These
men did not command the regular citizen army of legions, but rather
whatever forces they could hastily conscript on the spot, since the
Romans did not yet consider this a real war but rather the raids and
the predations of bandits. When they attacked Spartacus, however, they

---

[1]Appian is confused, and not for the first time. The praetor sent out was Gaius
Claudius Glaber. Appian has conflated his name with that of another praetor, Publius
Varinius; Publius Valerius, otherwise unattested, is perhaps Appian's way of referring to
Publius Varinius.

---

Appian, *Roman History: The Civil Wars,* 1.14.116–21.

were defeated. Spartacus even captured Varinius's own horse right from under him. The commander of the Romans was that close to being taken prisoner by a gladiator.

After this debacle, many more men came to join Spartacus, and his army soon numbered seventy thousand.[2] He had regular weapons forged for them, and he began to collect basic supplies for an army. Meanwhile, in the city of Rome, the Romans dispatched the two consuls with two legions under their command. Of these two armies, one defeated Crixus, who was in command of thirty thousand men, in the Garganus Mountains. Two-thirds of Crixus's army perished along with Crixus himself. Spartacus, by contrast, exerted great efforts to make his way through the Apennine mountains to the Alps and then to the land of the Gauls on the other side of the Alps. One of the consuls got to the place before him and prevented his escape, while the other consul harried the rearguard of Spartacus's army. Spartacus turned on them one after the other, however, and defeated each Roman army in turn, with the result that the Romans were forced to flee from the field of battle in great confusion and uproar.

As an offering to the dead, Spartacus sacrificed 300 Roman prisoners on behalf of Crixus. With the 120,000 men under his command, he began a march on Rome. So that traveling would be as light as possible, he torched all unnecessary supplies, killed all prisoners of war, and slaughtered all pack animals. Many deserters from the Roman army came to him, but he accepted none of them. The consuls made a stand against him in a place in the land of Picenum. Another great armed struggle took place here, and the Romans were defeated again. Spartacus changed his mind about an attack on Rome. He decided that he was not ready for an all-out battle and that his whole army was not yet properly armed for regular warfare. Moreover, so far no city had come over to his side, but only slaves, deserters, and the flotsam and jetsam of humanity. He therefore decided to occupy the mountains around Thurii instead. Indeed, he even captured the city of Thurii itself.

Spartacus did not permit merchants to import gold and silver, and he forbade his own men to acquire any. For the most part, he purchased iron and copper and did not censure those who imported these metals. For this reason, the slaves had large quantities of basic materials and were well supplied and able to stage frequent raids. When they next entered into hand-to-hand combat with the Romans, they defeated the Romans again and returned to their base heavily laden with booty.

---

[2]For this number, as for most of those that follow, Appian is counting in large, general numerical units of myriads, or ten thousands, and is therefore not giving exact figures.

This was now the third year of a war that had become particularly fearful for the Romans, although at the beginning they had treated it as a laughing matter and a contemptible thing, since it involved only gladiators. When it came time to hold the selection of new commands for the praetors, a morbid fear seized all the men, and not one of them would proffer his name for the position. Finally, [Marcus] Licinius Crassus, a man renowned among the Romans for his birth and wealth, was appointed to the command and marched forth with six freshly recruited legions. When Crassus arrived in the campaign theater, he added the two legions of the consuls to his own. Since the men in the old units had been defeated so often in combat with Spartacus, Crassus selected every tenth man from the consular legions by lot and had him executed. Some say that Crassus himself went with his new army into battle and was defeated, and that it was only then that he selected every tenth man from the entire army by lot. If the latter story is true, it means that four thousand men were involved, and that even the very large number of men whom he had to execute did not deter Crassus. Whatever Crassus actually did, he made himself more fearful than the enemy to his own men. He soon defeated a force of ten thousand of Spartacus's men who had made a camp by themselves, destroying two-thirds of them. He then marched with great confidence against Spartacus himself. Crassus defeated Spartacus and pursued him with lightning speed to the seacoast, where Spartacus was preparing to sail to Sicily. Thus trapping Spartacus, Crassus cut a trench, constructed a defensive wall, and erected sharp stake works along its entire line.

On the day when Spartacus tried to force a breakout and make a dash for Samnite territory, Crassus killed about six thousand of Spartacus's supporters in the early morning and another similar number toward the twilight hours. Only three men from the Roman army died and seven were wounded, so great was the change in the soldiers' eagerness for victory because of their recent punishment. Spartacus, who was awaiting the arrival of additional cavalry, remained where he was and no longer ventured into battle with his whole army. Rather, he staged sudden, small-scale attacks on his besiegers at selected points, here and there, hitting them suddenly and sharply. He had his men throw bundles of branches into the trench and set them on fire, which made the going very difficult for those who were engaged in this task. He crucified a Roman prisoner in this middle ground as a visual demonstration to his own men of what would happen to them if they did not win. When the Romans in the city [of Rome] learned of Crassus's siege tactics, they thought it unworthy that this war against the gladiators should be prolonged much longer. As an additional force, they enlisted the army of Pompey, who had just arrived back from Spain. The Romans had come to accept that dealing with Spartacus would be a very difficult and substantial undertaking.

When he heard of this measure, Crassus strove in every possible way to force a confrontation with Spartacus, in order to prevent the glory of winning the war from falling to Pompey. Thinking that he might take advantage of Pompey's arrival, Spartacus offered to negotiate an agreement with Crassus. When his proposal was disdainfully rejected, Spartacus decided to make one last desperate attempt. Since his cavalry had now arrived, he made a charge directly through the line of Crassus's wall and ditch with his entire army. Spartacus then marched quickly in the direction of Brundisium, with Crassus in hot pursuit. But when he learned that [Lucius Licinius] Lucullus, who had just returned victorious from his war against Mithridates, was disembarking his army at Brundisium, Spartacus fell into total despair. With no other choice before him, Spartacus wheeled around his still large and substantial army to force a direct confrontation with Crassus.

Since so many tens of thousands of desperate men were involved, the result was a protracted battle of epic proportions. Spartacus took a spear wound in his thigh. Collapsing on one knee, he held his shield up in front of him and fought off those who were attacking him, until he and the large number of men around him were finally surrounded and cut down. The rest of his army was thrown into disarray and confusion and was slaughtered in huge numbers. The killing was on such a scale that it was not possible to count the dead. The Romans lost about a thousand men. The body of Spartacus was never found. When the survivors among Spartacus's men, who were still a large number, fled from the battle, they went up into the mountains, where they were pursued by Crassus's forces. Splitting themselves into four groups, they continued to fight until all of them had perished—all, that is, except six thousand of them, who were taken prisoner and crucified along the whole length of the highway that ran from Capua to Rome.[3]

Crassus accomplished this feat within six months. The result was the sudden emergence of a bitter competition for honor between Pompey and him.

---

[3]Presumably, the Appian Way. The distance was about 125 miles, so there would have been one body of a crucified slave raised on a cross every 35 to 40 yards along the entire distance of the road.

# 61

## APPIAN

# King Mithridates of Pontus and Spartacus

### Second Century C.E.

*In this passage, Appian is speaking of King Mithridates, who, during his war against the Romans, was trying to entice the Gauls into an attack on Italy in 64 B.C.E.*

He knew that almost all of Italy had recently revolted from the Romans because of the hatred the Italians had for them, that the Italians had fought a protracted war against the Romans, and that they had sided with the gladiator Spartacus against the Romans, even though he was a wholly disreputable person.

Appian, *Roman History: The Mithridatic War,* 109.519–20.

# 62

## SALLUST

# The Spartacus War

### First Century B.C.E.

*Of the historians who preserved extended accounts of the war, Sallust must be deemed the most important, in part because he was the closest in time to the events themselves. The fragments of Sallust's history that are translated here are arranged according to the edition by the German scholar Bertold Maurenbrecher. For a different order, and meaning, see Patrick McGushin, Sallust: The Histories, 2 vols. (Oxford, 1992). Not all of the fragments are translated here, since many of them are too brief to be of much use and their placement in the temporal sequence of events is too questionable.*

Sallust, *Histories,* Book 3, fragments 90–94, 96–102, 106; Book 4, fragments 22–23, 25, 30–33, 37, 40–41.

Spartacus, the leader of the gladiators, was one of the seventy-four men who escaped from the gladiatorial school and waged a major war against the Roman people. . . .

. . . He [Spartacus] was a man of immense bodily strength and spirit.

. . . [Spartacus and his men] reached the foot of the mountain [probably Vesuvius].

. . . if they were to meet resistance, they should prefer to die by steel than to perish by hunger. . . .

. . . Cossinius was washing himself in the spring at a nearby villa.

*[The manuscript of the following fragment is too fragmented to note all the breaks in detail here. Only the major breaks are noted.]*

. . . and they fired [the tips of their wooden spears?] so that in addition to having the appearance necessary for war, they would be no less dangerous than if they were made of iron. While the fugitive slaves were busy with these tasks, [Publius] Varinius sent his quaestor Gaius Thoranius [Toranius] to Rome so that the people there might be able to get a truthful report about how matters actually stood from someone who had witnessed them. Some of his soldiers were ill because of the bad autumn weather, and none of those soldiers who had been defeated in the last battle, and who had run away, had returned to their units despite the harsh orders issued by Varinius that they were to do so. The rest of the soldiers—in an act that was the height of disgraceful behavior—were simply refusing to do their duty. With four thousand of the soldiers who were still willing to follow orders [or, who were volunteers?], Varinius established his camp—which was well defended with a wall, trench, and large-scale fortification—close to the camp of the rebellious slaves.

Since they had used up their own food supplies, all the fugitive slaves silently departed from their camp at about the second hour of the night watch. To avoid a surprise attack from the Romans while they were away raiding the countryside, the rebels, according to regular army practice, usually appointed night watchmen and guards and assigned the other usual duties. This time they left behind only a trumpet signaler in the camp. Then they propped up fresh corpses on stakes at the gates of the camp, so that those who saw them from afar would be led to believe that night guards had been stationed. They lit many fires in their camp so that by causing fear to . . . Varinius's [men?], they might flee . . . and . . . *[the manuscript is defective]* themselves went off on out-of-the-way tracks. . . . *[the manuscript is defective]*

When it was well after dawn, Varinius noticed the absence of the insults usually shouted by the slaves and the showers of stones with which the fugitives used to pelt his camp, and, in addition, the lack of noise and shouting from the enemy that used to strike him from all directions. He therefore ordered his cavalry to the top of a hill that overlooked the surrounding countryside to discover the whereabouts of the fugitive slaves and to hurry to follow their tracks. Although he believed that the slaves were by now far away, he still withdrew his men into a defensive formation, fearing an ambush, so that he could double the strength of his force with new recruits. . . . *[the manuscript is defective]*

Some days later, contrary to their usual behavior, our soldiers became more confident, and their tongues began to wag boastfully. For this reason, and not having learned from his own earlier experiences, Varinius rashly led his new and inexperienced soldiers, along with his other troops who were already demoralized by the defeats previously suffered by others, at a quick march against the camp of the fugitive slaves. Now they marched in silence and with much less extravagant boasting than when they had earlier pressed for combat. At this same time, the slaves were quarreling among themselves about their plans and were close to an internal revolt. Crixus and his people, who were Gauls and Germans, wanted to march directly against the enemy, in order to force an armed confrontation. Spartacus, on the other hand, advised a different course. . . . *[the manuscript is defective]*

. . . they happened on peasant farmers from Abella who were keeping watch over their fields. . . .

*[The manuscript of the following fragment is too fragmented to note all the defects in detail. Only the major breaks are noted.]*

. . . [It seemed?] to others and to him [Spartacus] . . . that they should not [wander around aimlessly lest?] . . . they be hemmed in on all sides and slaughtered to the last man. . . . Therefore, it was necessary to leave the place as quickly as possible. A few of the slaves, who were prudent men and who had free and noble minds. . . praised [his advice?] and held that they ought to do what Spartacus was suggesting. Some slaves were stupid and foolishly had confidence in the large numbers who were flooding in to join their movement and in their own ferocity, while others shamefully forgot all about [returning to?] their homelands. But the vast majority of the fugitives, because of their servile nature, thought of nothing but blood and booty. . . .

... [Spartacus's] plan ... seemed to be the best one. Then he persuaded them to move down into the lowland plains, which were rich in cattle, where they would be able to increase their number with select men of high quality before the arrival of Varinius with his newly refreshed army. A good guide was quickly found from among the prisoners taken from the Picentini. Spartacus made his way stealthily through the Eburian Hills [Eboli Mountains] and reached Nares in Lucania.[1] At daybreak, he arrived at Forum Annii, without having been discovered by the local farmers. Contrary to the orders of their general, the fugitive slaves immediately began to rape young girls and married women, while others ...

... [cut down] those who tried to resist them and who were trying to escape, inflicting wounds on them in a depraved manner, when their backs were turned, and left in their trail the torn bodies of the half-dead persons. Others threw firebrands onto the roofs of houses. Many slaves in the town were by nature sympathetic allies and uncovered things that their masters had hidden away or dragged out the masters themselves from their hiding places. Nothing was either too sacred or too wicked to be spared the rage of these barbarians and their servile characters. Spartacus himself was powerless to stop them, even though he repeatedly entreated them to stop and even attempted by sending on swift messengers. . . . But the slaves [were] intent on their cruel slaughter, . . . and after having stayed there for that day and the following night, and having doubled the number of fugitive slaves, he broke camp at dawn and established his position in a wide plain, where he watched the local farmers leaving their houses for work — it was the time of year when the autumn harvests were ripening in the fields.

When broad daylight came, the inhabitants realized from their neighbors, who were on the run, that the fugitive slaves were approaching, and so they fled with all of their possessions. . . . *[the manuscript is defective]*

There was one man in the rural region of Lucania by the name of Publipor [Publius's Boy, a slave name], who was knowledgeable about the place. . . .

... No place in the region would be safe for them, unless they had occupied it in force. . . .

... They stripped [the dead] of their arms and their horses. . . .

---

[1]Nares Lucanae (literally, the Lucanian Nostrils), a narrow pass that connected southern Campania with northern Lucania (Map 4).

. . . these men [those coming to join Spartacus's forces] were very knowledgeable about the region and were used to making woven baskets from branches for their farmwork. Because of their lack of real shields, they used this same knowledge to make small circular shields for themselves like those used by cavalrymen.

At the same time, [Gnaeus Cornelius] Lentulus ordered his men to form a double battle line on a commanding height of land and defended it, but with heavy losses to his own forces. . . .

Those men who had been selected by lot, he had taken out and beaten to death. . . .

. . . all of Italy is attenuated into the extremities formed by the two peninsulas of Bruttium and Sallentinum. . . .

. . . and that part of Italy that stretches out in the direction of Sicily is entered by a corridor that is not wider than thirty-five miles. . . .

When hollow jars were placed beneath the planks, they were lashed together with vine tendrils or strips of leather hide. . . .

. . . when the rafts became entangled, they impeded the arrival of help. . . .

Gaius Verres strengthened the fortifications on the shores [of Sicily] closest to Italy. . . .

. . . they were now in the forest of Sila. . . .

. . . they began to argue among themselves and not to plan together. . . .

. . . in the meantime, just before daybreak, two Gallic women, avoiding contact with the group, climbed up into the mountains to spend their menstrual periods there.[2] . . .

. . . he [Spartacus] was finally killed, not easily nor unavenged. . . .

All of the documents that follow are minor sources for the history of the Spartacus slave war.

---

[2]This must be the same incident alluded to by Plutarch ". . . two women who were making ritual sacrifices on behalf of the enemy spotted them" (see page 129). Either Plutarch misunderstood the original Latin or deliberately bowdlerized the text.

# 63

## LIVY

# A Brief Account of the Beginning of the War in 73 B.C.E.

### First Century B.C.E.

*The historian Livy, in an excerpt from his general history of Rome, reports the beginnings of the Spartacus slave war.*

Seventy-four gladiators escaped from the school of Lentulus [Batiatus] at Capua, and, collecting a large number of ordinary slaves as well as those kept in slave barracks, they began to wage a war under their leaders, Crixus and Spartacus. They defeated the legate Claudius Pulcher and the praetor Publius Varenus[1] in battle.

[1]The commanders were Gaius Claudius Glaber as praetor and then Publius Varinius.

Livy, *Summaries*, 95.

# 64

## LIVY

# A Brief Account of the Events of 73–72 B.C.E.

### First Century B.C.E.

*The historian Livy, in an excerpt from his general history of Rome, reports events in the Spartacus slave war.*

The praetor Quintus Arrius killed Crixus, the general of the fugitive slaves, along with twenty thousand of his men. The consul Gnaeus [Cornelius] Lentulus fought unsuccessfully against Spartacus. The consul Lucius Gellius [Publicola] and the praetor Quintus Arrius were

Livy, *Summaries*, 96.

defeated in battle by this same Spartacus. . . . The proconsul Gaius Cassius [Longinus] and the praetor Gnaeus Manlius also fought against Spartacus, but with no success. The conduct of the war was therefore assigned to the praetor Marcus [Licinius] Crassus.

# 65

# LIVY

# A Brief Account of the End of the War in 71 B.C.E.

## First Century B.C.E.

*The historian Livy, in an excerpt from his general history of Rome, reports the end of the Spartacus war.*

The praetor Marcus Crassus first fought a successful engagement with that part of the fugitive slaves made up of Gauls and Germans. He killed thirty-five thousand of the enemy, along with their leaders Castus and Gannicus. He then defeated Spartacus, killing Spartacus along with sixty thousand of his men.

Livy, *Summaries,* 97.

# 66

# EUTROPIUS

# A Brief Account of the Spartacus Slave War

## First Century B.C.E.

*Eutropius provides a brief summary of the big events affecting Rome in the year 73 B.C.E. He probably derived most of his information from the*

Eutropius, *A Brief Survey of Roman History,* 6.7.

*lost books of Livy covering these same events [that is, the same source used by Orosius in Document 67].*

---

In the six hundred and seventy-eighth year of the foundation of the City (73 B.C.E.), Marcus Licinius Lucullus, the cousin of the Lucullus who was waging war against Mithridates, received Macedonia as his province. And a new war suddenly broke out in Italy itself. Seventy-four gladiators under the leadership of Spartacus, Crixus and Oenomaus broke out of the gladiatorial school at Capua and made their escape. Wandering through Italy, they raised no less serious a war than Hannibal had. For after many generals and, along with them, two consuls of the Romans, had been defeated, they [the rebel slaves] gathered together an army of almost 60,000 armed men. They were defeated in Apulia by Marcus Licinius Crassus, the proconsul. Only after many disasters had been suffered by Italy, an end was finally put to this war in its third year.

# 67

## OROSIUS

### *An Account of the Opening and Closing Phases of the War*

#### *Fifth Century C.E.*

---

*The Christian priest and historian Orosius, writing in the fifth century but drawing on the lost books of Livy, provides some brief notices on the war.*

---

In the 679th year from the founding of the city of Rome, the year in which [Marcus Terentius Varro] Lucullus and [Gaius] Cassius [Longinus] were consuls [73 B.C.E.], sixty-four slaves escaped from Gnaeus Lentulus's school for gladiators at Capua. Led by the Gauls Crixus and

---

Orosius, *History against the Pagans,* 5.24.1–8, 18–19.

Oenomaus and by the Thracian Spartacus, the fugitives moved immediately to occupy Mount Vesuvius. From there, they rushed out and captured the army camp of the praetor Clodius [Claudius Glaber], who had surrounded them and placed them under siege. Once they had put him to flight, they carried off everything as plunder. Passing by Consentia and Metapontum,[1] the slaves soon attracted a large armed following. It is reported that Crixus had a huge gathering of ten thousand men under his command and that Spartacus led a force three times that large. These were now the two leaders, since Oenomaus had been killed in an earlier battle.

Wherever they went, the slaves indiscriminately mixed slaughter, arson, theft, and rape. At the funeral rites of a woman whom they had taken prisoner and who had committed suicide because of her anguish over the violation of her sexual honor, they staged gladiatorial games, using four hundred prisoners they had taken. Those who had once been the spectacle were now to be the spectators: It was as gladiatorial entrepreneurs rather than as military commanders that they staged these games.

After this, the consuls [Lucius] Gellius [Publicola] and [Gnaeus Cornelius] Lentulus [Clodianus] [72 B.C.E.] were dispatched with armies to fight the rebellious slaves. Gellius defeated Crixus in battle, although Crixus put up a savage resistance. Lentulus was defeated by Spartacus and ran from the field of battle. The armies of both consuls were merged, but in vain, since they suffered another severe defeat and ran from the field of battle. Then the proconsul Gaius Cassius [Longinus] was likewise defeated in the fighting and killed by Spartacus. Terror spread through the city of Rome, just as it had in the time when Hannibal had threatened its gates.

The senate immediately dispatched Marcus [Licinius] Crassus in the command of the consular legions and with new reinforcements. Crassus then engaged the fugitive slaves in battle. He killed 6,000 of them and took only 900 prisoners. Before advancing to attack the forces commanded by Spartacus, who was setting up his camp close to the head of the Silarus River, Crassus destroyed Spartacus's Gallic and German auxiliaries, killing 30,000 men along with their commanders. Only last of all did Crassus strike Spartacus himself, who was advancing to engage him with his battle lines ready and who had the largest number of the fugitive slaves with him. It is reported that 60,000 men were killed and 6,000 were taken prisoner, and that 3,000 Roman citizens were taken back. Still others, who had survived the battle and who were wandering about the countryside, were gradually eliminated by means of a thorough hunt for them made by a large number of our army commanders.

---

[1]*Consentia and Metapontum:* the modern-day cities of Cosenza and Metaponto.

*[At the end of the fifth book of his history, Orosius compares the significance of the great wars of the late Roman Republic—those against Jugurtha, Mithridates, and Sertorius—with the Spartacus slave war.]*

When the war in Spain against Sertorius had not yet been brought to an end, and indeed Sertorius himself was still alive, this war against the fugitive slaves—or rather, to describe it more accurately, this war against the gladiators—was the cause of terrible horrors. It was not a mere spectacle reserved for the sight of a few but was the cause of universal fear. Just because it is called a war against fugitive slaves should not mislead: The war should not be considered a mean[2] and worthless thing just because of its name. During its course, individual consuls were frequently defeated badly, and sometimes both consuls who joined their armies into a single force—in vain—were defeated. And very many Roman nobles were killed. As for the fugitive slaves themselves, the number of them who were slaughtered in the war surpassed 100,000.

# 68

## VELLEIUS PATERCULUS

# A Brief Synopsis of the Spartacus War

### First Century *C.E.*

*Velleius Paterculus, writing his history of Rome under the second emperor Tiberius, in the early first century C.E., tells of the Spartacus war.*

While the war against Sertorius was being fought in Spain, sixty-four runaway slaves under the leadership of Spartacus escaped from a gladiatorial school at Capua. Seizing weapons from Capua, they first made their way to Mount Vesuvius. Then, as their number grew with each passing day, they inflicted serious and widespread damage on Italy. Their number increased to such an extent that when they entered the

---

[2]*mean:* worthy of little regard.

Velleius Paterculus, *History of Rome,* 2.30.5–6.

final battle, they had 241,000[1] men with which to oppose the Roman army. The glory for the victory was reaped by Marcus [Licinius] Crassus, who then, by the consensus of all, became the leading man in the state.

# 69

## FLORUS

# A Detailed Synopsis of the Spartacus War

### Second Century C.E.

---

*In the first sentence, Florus is referring to his earlier account of the two slave wars on the island of Sicily (Documents 40 and 54). This is the "shame of slaves in arms" to which he is referring.*

---

One is able to endure even the shame of slaves in arms. For although slaves are persons who have been made subject to punishment in every possible way by some stroke of misfortune, they are still a type of human being, albeit an inferior type, and they are capable of being initiated into the benefits of the freedom that we enjoy. But I do not know what to call the war that was incited under the leadership of Spartacus. For when slaves served as soldiers and gladiators were their army commanders—the former the lowest sort of men, and the latter the worst—they simply added mockery to the disaster itself.

Spartacus, Crixus, and Oenomaus escaped from the gladiatorial training school of Lentulus [Batiatus] with thirty or more men who shared their misfortune, and rushed out of the town of Capua. Calling for slaves to flock to their standards, they soon collected more than ten thousand men. Not satisfied with having made their escape, they also wished to avenge themselves. The first place that attracted them, as if it

---

[1]The number in the manuscript is corrupt.

---

Florus, "The War against Spartacus," in *A Synopsis of Roman History,* 2.8.1–14.

were an altar of the goddess Venus,[1] was Mount Vesuvius. When they were placed under siege there by Clodius [Claudius] Glaber, the slaves let themselves down through a crevice in the mountain by means of ropes woven from wild vine tendrils and made their way to its very foot. Then, by way of a hidden egress, they launched a surprise attack on the unsuspecting Roman general and captured his camp. Next they captured other Roman army camps, including that of Varenius [Varinius] and then that of Thoranius [Toranius]. They rampaged over the whole of Campania. Not satisfied with destroying rural villas and villages, they devastated the towns of Nola, Nuceria, Thurii, and Metapontum, inflicting a terrible slaughter on them in the process.

With the daily arrival of new recruits, they were finally able to form themselves into a regular army. They made rough shields for themselves out of vine branches covered with animal hides, and swords and spears by melting down and recasting their [leg] irons from the slave barracks. And so that they should lack nothing required by a real army, they put together a cavalry force by taming wild horses that they happened to come across, and they took to their own leader the insignia and ceremonial bundles of rods and axes that they had captured from the Roman commanders. These were not refused by the man who had begun his life as a regularly paid soldier in Thrace, was next an army deserter, then a bandit, and finally—a tribute to his bodily strength—a gladiator. He celebrated the deaths of his generals who had died in battle with funerary rituals usually reserved for regular army commanders. He ordered prisoners of war that his armies had captured to fight one another around the funeral pyres, hoping to demonstrate, I suppose, that he could expiate all his past shame by transforming himself into an exhibitor of gladiatorial contests. After this, he launched attacks on full consular armies and obliterated the army of Lentulus in the Apennine mountains and the army camp of Gaius Crassus near Mutina. Elated by these victories, he actually considered—which is shameful enough for us—an attack on the city of Rome itself.

Finally, the combined resources of our empire rose up against this heavy-armored gladiator, and [Marcus] Licinius Crassus preserved our Roman honor. When the slaves had been defeated and driven from the field of battle by Crassus, the enemy (it shames me actually to call them this) took refuge in the remotest parts of Italy. Hemmed into a corner of Bruttium, they prepared to make their escape to Sicily. Since they did

---

[1]Perhaps the best suggestion for the Latin text, which is corrupt at this point. "Altars of Venus" were known as places of asylum for escaped slaves.

not have ships to take them, they tried to cross the swift-moving waters of the strait between the mainland and the island by using rafts made of wooden beams and barrels lashed together with thin vine tendrils, but in vain. In a final effort, they attempted a breakout and met with a death worthy of real men. As was appropriate for men commanded by a gladiator, they fought to the very end with no release from their fate.[2] Spartacus himself died fighting bravely at the front of his men, just like a true general.

[2]A gladiator who had fought a good fight was, as a reward, let off, or excused, by the judges of the contest to fight another day. This did not happen here.

# 70

## ATHENAEUS

## *A Brief Synopsis of the Spartacus War*

### *Second Century C.E.*

*Athenaeus, a Greek compiler of various facts, here includes some odd facts concerning the Spartacus war.*

The gladiator Spartacus, who became a fugitive from the Italian city of Capua about the time of the wars with Mithridates, incited a very large number of slaves to revolt. He himself was a slave, a Thracian by origin. The slaves overran the whole of Italy for a long time. Large numbers of slaves hurried to join him every day. If he had not been killed in the battle that he fought against [Marcus] Licinius Crassus, he would have caused no small amount of "sweat" to my fellow citizens, just as Eunus did in Sicily.[1]

[1]It is unclear what the Greek *idrota* or "sweat" means—it could mean either to cause a lot of hard work or a sense of terrible fright.

Athenaeus, *Deipnosophistae,* 6.272f–73a.

# 71

## VARRO

# Spartacus Becomes a Gladiator
### First Century B.C.E.

*In a lost work by Varro, a Roman agricultural writer of the first century B.C.E., there was a reference to Spartacus.*

Although he was an innocent man, Spartacus was condemned to a gladiatorial school[1] [or to the professional life of a gladiator?].

Sosipater Charisius, 1.133 (ed. Keil).

# 72

## DIODORUS SICULUS

# Spartacus as a Good Man
### First Century B.C.E.

*The historian Diodorus Siculus provides a brief synopsis of the character of Spartacus.*

Spartacus the barbarian, having been done a favor by someone, showed himself to be grateful to the man. For even among barbarians, human nature is self-taught to return an equal favor to those who bestow benefits on us.

[1]The words *ad gladiatorium* (to the gladiatorial school) are a conjecture by the historian Niebuhr.

Diodorus Siculus, *Library of History,* 38/39.21.

# 73

## FRONTINUS

# Stratagems Used by Spartacus against the Romans

### First Century C.E.

*A Roman senator who wrote works on aqueducts and on military tactics, Frontinus here includes examples of various subterfuges used by Spartacus in his battles with Roman forces.*

During the night Spartacus filled up the trench, by which he had been hemmed in by Marcus Crassus, with the bodies of prisoners and of herd animals, and in this way managed to cross over it. This same man [that is, Spartacus], when he was besieged on that part of Mount Vesuvius which is the harshest and which was therefore not closely guarded, wove together chains made from wild willow branches. Climbing down by means of these, he not only escaped but was able to terrify Clodius so much from the other side [of the mountain] that not a few Roman army cohorts gave way before seventy-four gladiators. And the same man, when he was cut off by the [forces of the] proconsul Publius Varinius, fixed dead bodies on stakes that he had set up at small intervals before the gate of his camp, furnishing them with clothing and weapons. To those who looked [at Spartacus's camp] from a distance, these [bodies] looked like a set of camp guards. In addition, he lit fires throughout the whole of his camp. Fooling the enemy with this empty display, he led his troops out in the silence of the night. . . .

Shields were manufactured for Spartacus and his troops with willow branches that were covered with leather. . . .

In the war with the fugitive slaves, Crassus fortified two camps at Cantenna close to the camp of the enemy. He moved his troops into action at night. So that the enemy might be deceived, he left his command headquarters in the larger camp. Crassus himself led out his troops and established them at the base of the aforementioned mountain. Dividing up his cavalry, he ordered Lucius Quintius to confront the part [of the slave forces] led by Spartacus and to keep him occupied in combat.

Frontinus, *Strategies,* 1.5.20, 1.7.6, 2.5.34

The other part [of the slave forces], the Gauls and Germans of Castus and Cannicus, he [Quintius] was to lure into combat by drawing them away by a pretended flight to the place where Crassus had set out his battle line. When the barbarians had pursued them and when the cavalry retreated to the wings, the Roman battle line suddenly showed itself and rushed forward with a great clamor. Livy says that 35,000 armed men were killed in this battle along with their officers, five Roman "eagles" were reclaimed, along with twenty-six battle standards and a great amount of booty, in which were five *fasces* [bundles of ceremonial rods] with their axes.

## 74

## CICERO

# Roman Governor Verres Faces the Threat Posed by Spartacus

### First Century B.C.E.

*The young orator Cicero, who prosecuted Gaius Verres, the Roman governor of Sicily, on charges of extorting money and goods from his provincial subjects, is attempting here to blacken Verres's reputation. He does this by calling into question Verres's governorship of Sicily in the years 73–71 B.C.E., precisely when the Spartacus slave war was raging on the mainland of southern Italy, directly opposite the island. Given the previous Sicilian slave wars, there was a reasonable fear that the slaves in Sicily might rebel again. Verres seems to have taken the appropriately savage repressive measures needed to keep the island under control (successfully, from the Roman point of view). But Cicero belittles this achievement, significantly managing never to mention Spartacus by name in his attack on Verres's administration.*

What are you saying? That Sicily was freed from a war of fugitive slaves by your brave actions? A deed deserving of great praise and an honorable oration—but for what war? We have always accepted the fact that after the war that Manius Aquillius brought to an end, there

Cicero, *Against Verres,* 2.5.5–6.

were no more slave wars in Sicily. But, you say, there *was* one in Italy. I agree. And it was a great and violent war. But surely you're not trying to claim some share of the praise that came from *it?* Surely you don't imagine that you're going to share the glory of that victory with Marcus [Licinius] Crassus or Gnaeus Pompeius [Pompey the Great]? Yes, I suppose that your arrogance is of a scale that you would actually dare to say something of that sort. You would have us believe that you were able to prevent bands of fugitive slaves from crossing over from Italy into Sicily? Where? When? From what direction? Did they attempt their landing with rafts or real ships? I've never heard anything of this sort. But I have heard that the energetic actions and planning of Marcus Crassus, that bravest of men, prevented the fugitive slaves from lashing rafts together, with the result that they were not able to cross over to Messana. Indeed, if there had been any guard posts positioned in Sicily against their attack, there would not have been such a great effort to prevent them from making the attempt. But even if there was a war in Italy so close to Sicily, nevertheless there was no war in Sicily itself. What's the surprise? For when there was a slave war in Sicily, which is separated from Italy by the same distance, none of it penetrated across into Italy. Why [are you] suggesting to us the closeness of the lands to each other at this place? To impute that there was easy access for our enemies or that there was a danger of the infection spreading through imitation of the war? Without the advantage of ships, however, any chance of entry into Sicily for such men was not just temporarily blocked but so completely closed off that you would have to say that it would have been easier for them to get to the shores of the Atlantic Ocean than to Cape Peloris [on the northeastern tip of Sicily].

## 75

## CICERO

# *Verres Represses Slave Conspiracies on Sicily*
### *First Century B.C.E.*

What then? Were there no slave rebellions in Sicily when Verres was governor, and were no conspiracies of slaves formed? Certainly nothing that was reported to the Senate and the Roman people — nothing which

Cicero, *Against Verres,* 2.5.9–20.

that man wrote in any official communication sent to Rome. Nonetheless, I suspect that servile uprisings did begin to be formed in several places in Sicily. I am led to suspect this not so much from any specific events themselves as from the deeds and decrees of *that man* [Verres] when he was governor. And remember that I am *not* moved by any hostile intent. I am simply bringing to your attention and putting on record those matters that Verres himself will try to establish later [in this trial] and that you jurors, therefore, have not yet heard.

In the region of Triocala [Triokala], the same city the fugitive slaves occupied in an earlier time, the slaves owned by a Sicilian named Leonidas were suspected of forming a conspiracy. The matter was reported to *that man*. And, as is indeed right and proper, by his order the men who had been named were immediately arrested and taken to Lilybaeum. The matter was reported to their master, a trial was held, and the men were found guilty. What then? What do you *think* happened next? Perhaps you might expect outright theft or plunder? No—you don't always have to look for the same thing in all situations involving *that man*. After all, what chance is there for theft in the midst of a war scare? And if there was any opportunity for him to acquire a gain in this matter, it was passed by. Verres was able to extort some money from Leonidas, when he ordered the man to present himself. A sort of deal was struck—which for *that man* wouldn't have been anything new—that they wouldn't hear the case. There was, however, another way: The men who had been convicted could be acquitted! But what basis was there for plunder, when the slaves had already been found guilty? They had to be taken to their execution. Those who were in the governor's judicial council were witness to the facts, the court records were witness, the resplendent city of Lilybaeum was witness, as was the honest and powerful local organization of Roman citizens. Nothing could be done. The slaves had to be led to execution. And so they were bound to the stake.

Even now, gentlemen of the jury, I see that you are looking at me expectantly, asking yourselves what happened next—a reasonable expectation since *that man* never did anything without at least some profit and rake-off for himself. So what sort of thing could be pulled off? Dream up whatever you think likely under the circumstances—as wicked a crime as you can imagine. I tell you, I'll surpass every one of your imaginings. These men—condemned for the crime of conspiracy, led off to their punishment, and tied to the stake—were suddenly, before the eyes of thousands of spectators, set free and returned to their master at Triocala.

What can *you* say to this—you raving madman—unless it is that which I do not ask: the whole purpose of this sordid and underhanded act that is in no doubt. Although the answer is clear, the question at least ought to be asked: How much money did you accept, and in what way did you receive it? I leave all of this to you, and will spare you the worry of giving an answer. For I have no fear that anyone will believe that you attempted to perpetrate a crime for free—a crime for which no one but you would have accepted money to commit. I'm not going to say any more about your modes of thieving and plundering. What I really want to do is to question your glorious reputation as a military commander.

What do you say, you wonderful guardian and defender of our province? When you put these slaves on trial, your finding was that they were guilty of an intent to seize arms and to raise a war in Sicily, and so you issued a sentence that was in agreement with the opinion of your judicial council. But when the condemned men had been handed over for punishment, according to the tradition of our ancestors, you dared to snatch them from the very midst of death and set them free. Why did you do this? So that the crosses you had set up for the condemned slaves should perhaps be kept there and set aside for innocent Roman citizens? Only cities that have lost everything and that are completely desperate are accustomed to take the lethal final step of restoring condemned men to freedom, freeing men who are bound in chains, calling back exiles, and canceling judgments made by the courts. . . . But what happened in this case is hardly believable. The men set free here were slaves who were suddenly dismissed from the very scene of their punishment by the very man who had found them guilty—and these were slaves who had been condemned on the charge of committing a crime that threatened the lives and limbs of all free persons.

What a resplendent commander! One who ought to be compared not with Manius Aquillius, that man of exceeding bravery, but with a Paullus, a Scipio, a Marius![1] How much foresight he showed in the hour of fear and danger faced by the province! When he saw that the minds of the slaves in Sicily were teetering on the edge of rebellion because of the slave war in Italy, not one of them dared to move because he had instilled such a dreadful fear into them! He ordered them to be arrested. Who would not be riven with fear? He put their masters on trial. What is more fearful for a slave? He announces what he seems to have done.

[1]Lucius Aemilius Paullus, Publius Cornelius Scipio Africanus, and Gaius Marius were brilliant army commanders who had won great victories over some of Rome's formidable foreign enemies—the Macedonians, Carthaginians, and Germans.

He actually appears to have extinguished the fire that was beginning to spread with the suffering and deaths of only a few victims. What happens next? Whips and flaming torches and the other tools necessary for the extreme punishment of the condemned and as a deterrent for the others: the instruments of torture and the cross. But these men were freed from all these punishments. Who can doubt that he instilled in the minds of the slaves a terminal fear when they saw a governor so easygoing that the lives of slaves who had been condemned to death for the crime of conspiracy were redeemed — either from Verres himself or from the executioner who was acting as his intermediary?

What? You mean to say that you didn't do exactly this same thing in the case of Aristodamus from Apollonia? What? And also in that of Leon from Imachara? What then? Did your suspicions of slave unrest and even the threat of servile war lead you to a more diligent care for your province, or rather to find a new avenue for wicked profits for yourself? Eumenides, a noble and honorable man from the city of Halicyae, and a man of considerable wealth, had a slave farm manager who was arrested at your instigation. You then accepted 60,000 sesterces from Eumenides, the man's owner. How this was done was confirmed recently by Eumenides when he gave evidence under oath. But that's nothing. You extorted 600,000 sesterces from the *eques* Gaius Matrinius during his absence from Sicily while he was away at Rome, alleging that you had discovered that his slave farm managers and shepherds were forming a conspiracy. Lucius Flavius, who was the agent for Gaius Matrinius's business affairs and who counted out the money to you, gave testimony to this effect. So did Matrinius himself. And so did that most distinguished man, Gnaeus Lentulus, the censor, who for the sake of the esteem in which he held Matrinius, wrote a letter to you and had others write letters to you about the same matter.

What then? What about Apollonius, the son of Diocles, from the city of Panormus — who is also known by the Latin surname Geminus — how can we pass over his case? What other matter, indeed, is better known, the subject of more outrage, and more manifest throughout Sicily? When Verres came to Panormus, he ordered Apollonius to be summoned and hailed before his tribunal at the crowded and busy assizes[2] he was holding in the city. Men began to gossip with each other: "I'm surprised that Apollonius, a rich man, has remained untouched so long by that man." "He's certainly thought up something." "A rich man is not

---

[2]*assize:* a place where the Roman stopped on his tour of the province to hold court.

suddenly going to be summoned by Verres without a reason." There was a great sense of anticipation among these men about what was going to happen, when Apollonius himself ran up out of breath, accompanied by his younger son, since his elderly father had been bedridden for a long time.

In his formal charge, the governor named the slave who, he said, was Apollonius's master herdsman. Verres charged that this man was forming a conspiracy to incite the slaves owned by Apollonius to rebellion. But there was no such slave at all among Apollonius's slaves. Verres nonetheless ordered the man to be produced at once. Apollonius swore that he owned no such slave by that name. Verres then ordered Apollonius to be taken forcibly from his tribunal and to be thrown into prison. As he was being rushed away, the poor man cried out that he had done nothing wrong, that he had committed no crime, that all of his money was tied up on account and he had no liquid cash. It was when Apollonius shouted aloud these statements before the crowded assembly, in a manner in which anyone would be able to understand that he would not pay out any money, that he was manhandled with such severity. It was right at this juncture, I would like to emphasize, when he was shouting out loudly about the money, that he was thrown into chains.

Witness the hard determination of our governor! A governor who is being defended not just as any ordinary governor, but one who is being lauded as a supreme military commander. When a slave war was threatening, he freed condemned slaves from the same punishment that he then inflicted on innocent masters. Apollonius, a very wealthy man, who would lose his massive fortune if runaway slaves began a war in Sicily, is indicted on the charge of fomenting a slave war and is thrown into chains. And the slaves, whom Verres himself, in agreement with his judicial council, had found guilty on the charge of inciting a slave war, now, without seeking any advice from his council, were freed from all punishment on nothing but his own whim. . . . I shall not defend the case against Apollonius, my friend and guest host, and would not presume to rescind your judgment against him. And I will not be provoked into saying anything about this man's frugality, virtue, and diligence. I'm going to pass over the fact, which I've already mentioned, that his wealth consists of slaves, cattle, villas, and money on loan.

## 76

## CICERO

# *Execution of a Roman "Collaborator"*

### *First Century B.C.E.*

*In his prosecution of Gaius Verres, the governor of Sicily at the time of the Spartacus war, in 70 B.C.E., Cicero refers to harsh actions taken by Verres in the repression and punishment of persons whom he regarded as having collaborated with the rebel slaves.*

What am I to say, jurors, about Publius Gavius, a citizen of the municipality of Cosa? With what strength of voice, heaviness of words, and mental anguish should I speak? . . . I think that there is only one rational way: I will place the bare facts of the matter before you, a matter which is so serious that no special eloquence of mine is needed. . . . This Gavius about whom I am speaking . . . was thrown into chains by Verres . . . but somehow, I do not know how, he made his escape from the stone quarries [at Syracuse] and made his way to Messana . . . where he began to speak out, complaining that he, a Roman citizen, had been put in chains . . . when suddenly Verres ordered him to be arrested, to be stripped and bound in the middle of the forum, ordering that rods be brought out to beat him. The poor man shouted out that he was a Roman citizen and also a citizen of the municipality of Cosa . . . but Verres stated that he had learned that Gavius had been sent to Sicily by the leaders of the fugitive slaves [those led by Spartacus] for the purpose of spying . . . so Gavius was beaten with rods . . . and a cross was readied for the poor man. . . . I will produce witnesses who will testify that this is the very same man whom you, Verres, threw into the stone quarries at Syracuse. And I will produce citizens of Cosa who will testify . . . that the Publius Gavius whom you crucified was a Roman citizen and a citizen of the municipality of Cosa and *not* a spy for the runaway slaves . . . and you, Verres . . . admitted that Publius did shout out that he was a Roman citizen. But the word "citizen" did not have the least impact on you, did not cause you to have the smallest hesitation in your mind or to offer even a brief reprieve from the cruelest and most shameful of punishments [that is, crucifixion]. . . . In fact, you did not know who he was.

Cicero, *Verrines*, 2.5.158–70.

You only *suspected* that he was a spy. . . . What more do I need to say about Gavius? . . . What on earth was your purpose on having . . . his cross placed so that it looked toward the strait [of Messina, separating Italy and Sicily]? . . . You declared . . . that you chose to place the cross in that place so that this man, who was a Roman citizen, would see Italy from his cross . . . so that Italy might see her foster child murdered by an extreme and ultimate punishment that is fitting only for slaves . . . to be in the sight of Italy . . . on the direct route that everyone takes as they sail back and forth.

# 77

## AULUS GELLIUS

## *Marcus Crassus Celebrates His Victory over Spartacus*

### Second Century C.E.

*The second-century writer Aulus Gellius is describing the difference between the honor of an* ovatio *as opposed to the greater honor of a* triumph, *and uses Marcus Licinius Crassus as an example of the difference.*

The reason for awarding an *ovatio,* rather than a triumph, is either because a war was not proclaimed according to the proper rituals; because it was not fought with a real enemy; because the enemy had a humble and unworthy name, as in the case of slaves or pirates; or because the enemy's surrender was too quick and the victory was, as they say, "bloodless" and "without dust."

. . . so Marcus [Licinius] Crassus, when he had brought the war with the slaves to an end and had returned to Rome to celebrate an *ovatio,* disdainfully rejected the myrtle crown [of an *ovatio*] and used his influence to have a decree of the Senate passed that he was to be crowned with laurel, not with myrtle.[1]

[1]A general who celebrated a full-scale triumph rather than the lesser *ovatio* wore a crown of laurel leaves. Myrtle, which was used for the *ovatio,* was regarded as inferior.

Aulus Gellius, *Attic Nights,* 5.6.20–23.

# 78

## SUETONIUS

# Operations against Remnant Rebel Slaves of the Spartacus War in Southern Italy in the Late 60s B.C.E.

### Second Century C.E.

---

*The biographer Suetonius, in his biography of the first emperor Augustus, describes military operations taken by his father, Octavius, against groups of rebel slaves in southern Italy who were still causing troubles in the aftermath of the Spartacus war.*

---

After his praetorship [61 B.C.E.], Octavius[1] had the province of Macedonia assigned to him by lot. On the way out to govern his province, he destroyed the fugitive slaves who were remnants of the forces that had once fought for Spartacus and for Catiline, and who now were occupying the countryside around Thurii. This task was assigned to Octavius by the Senate as an additional special command. . . .

When he was an infant, Augustus was given the nickname "Thurinus" [the man from Thurii], either in remembrance of his ancestral parentage from the region or because, more recently, shortly after Augustus was born [63 B.C.E.], his father, Octavius, had conducted successful military operations against fugitive slaves in the region.

---

[1]Gaius Octavius, father of Augustus, the first Roman emperor.

---

Suetonius, *Life of Augustus,* 3.1, 7.1.

# List of the Principal Authors
# and Literary Sources

**Appian** (ca. 90s–160s C.E.) Appian was a Greek from Alexandria in Egypt. He acquired Roman citizenship and held a number of high-ranking posts in the bureaucracy of the Roman state in the early- to mid-second century C.E. under the emperors Hadrian and Antoninus Pius. In the 160s, Appian composed a history of Rome from its origins to his own day titled *Roman Affairs* (Romaika). It was arranged according to the ethnic groups the Romans confronted in their territorial expansion, with special emphasis on the wars they fought. Separate books were devoted to the civil wars that beleaguered the Roman state in the last generations of the Republic. It is important to note that Appian's *Civil Wars*, which includes the events of the Spartacus war, was written well over two centuries after the war itself. In composing his history, Appian seems to have depended on sources for the slave war similar to those used by Plutarch but different from those used by Sallust and Livy. Appian had much less of a command of Roman political institutions, dates, people, and geography than did the Latin historians of the same events.

**Athenaeus** (ca. 150–200 C.E.) Athenaeus was a Greek from the port city of Naucratis, in Egypt. Just before the year 200, he finished writing a very large polymorphous literary work called *The Philosophers' Feast* (Deipnosophistai) — a vast compilation of quotations from philosophers uttered during their dinner conversations. Not all of the compendium has survived. Some of the quotations are rather lengthy, and sometimes they are the only surviving records we have of earlier historical sources that are now lost.

**Aulus Gellius** (ca. 125–190? C.E.) Aulus Gellius's compendious collection of snippets of "interesting information" filled twenty books, titled *Attic Nights* (Noctes Atticae). This collection preserves many fragments of Latin literature that would otherwise have been lost.

**Caesar, Julius** (100–44 B.C.E.) Julius Caesar was the dominant political and military figure in the late Republic from the 50s B.C.E. until his assassination on the Ides of March, 44 B.C.E. He recounts his conquest of Gaul in the seven-book *Commentaries on the War in Gaul* (Commentarii de bello Gallico). In three books titled *On the Civil War* (De bello civili), he reports on the conflicts following his crossing of the Rubicon River in northern Italy in January 49 B.C.E. These wars were fought mainly against the adherents of his political rival Pompey the Great.

**Cassius Dio** (ca. 160s–230s C.E.) Cassius Dio was a wealthy senator from Nicaea, in the province of Bithynia, in the northwestern corner of present-day Turkey. In the last decades of his life, Dio served several Roman emperors, becoming consul and governor of important provinces of the Roman Empire. He composed an eighty-volume work titled *Roman Affairs* (Romaika) that covered events from the foundation of the city of Rome to his own day. Many parts of Dio's history have not survived intact. For the numerous passages that are quoted in this reader, we are dependent on much later synopses, which are little better than fragments torn from the original.

**Cato the Elder** (234–149 B.C.E.) Marcus Porcius Cato, also known as Cato the Elder, was a dominant political and cultural figure at the time of Rome's last wars against Carthage, its great rival in the western Mediterranean. During his long life (he died at age eighty-five, just as Rome's final war with Carthage began), Cato witnessed the massive transformation of Italy's rural economy. He came from Tusculum, an agricultural center about fifteen miles southeast of Rome. Throughout his life, he proclaimed the traditional ideal of the Roman citizen as a citizen farmer, which conflicted strongly with another side of Cato: a landholder who modernized his household to embrace the new commercialized agriculture, and who was consequently deeply involved in trade and commerce. As part of his devotion to Roman tradition and his own Latin culture, Cato provided many of the earliest texts in Latin prose, including the first largescale history in Latin and the first handbook devoted to the new slave-based agriculture, *On Agriculture* (De agricultural). The latter is the earliest extensive work in Latin prose that has survived.

**Cicero** (106–43 B.C.E.) Marcus Tullius Cicero was a great orator and senatorial politician of the last generation of the Roman Republic. He made a considerable reputation for himself when he was still young by conducting the prosecution of a fellow senator named Gaius Verres. Verres had been the governor of the Roman province of Sicily from 73 to 71 B.C.E. Because of formal complaints lodged against him by the Sicilians, Verres was put on trial on the charge of gross maladministration. In the trial of 70 B.C.E., Cicero insinuated that during Verres's governorship, which covered the same years as the Spartacus slave war in Italy, he had colluded with slave owners in much the same way an earlier governor had, which had been one of the main causes of the earlier slave wars in Sicily. Cicero's trial speeches, *Against Verres* (In Verrem), are an important source of Sicilian history during the years of the Spartacus war.

**Columella** (ca. mid-first century C.E.) Lucius Junius Moderatus Columella was a wealthy man of senatorial rank who came from the Roman municipality of Gades (now Cádiz) in southern Spain. His long life spanned at least the first six decades of the first century C.E. He was, therefore, a contemporary of his Spanish compatriot, the senator and philosopher Seneca. Like Cato and Varro before him, Columella, in his old age (probably in the 60s), composed a manual on slave-based farms titled *On Agriculture* (De Re Rustica) as well as a companion work titled *On Orchards* (De Arboribus). *On Agriculture* is the largest and most comprehensive surviving guide to the new Roman slave-based agriculture.

**Diodorus Siculus** (ca. 90s–40s B.C.E.) Diodorus "the Sicilian," who lived in the first century B.C.E., came from the city of Agyrion, in the Roman province of Sicily. He eventually left his home in Sicily to settle in the city of Rome, where he completed a forty-book general history of the world titled *The Library* (Bibliothêkê). He probably relied on an earlier history written by Posidonius for the events of the great slave wars in Sicily in the second century B.C.E. Only fifteen books of Diodorus's world history have survived. Unfortunately, those on the Sicilian slave wars have been lost. Only fragmentary quotations from them, which appear in sources written several centuries after his death, remain.

**Florus** (ca. 100–150 C.E.) Publius (?) Annaeus Florus was a Latin author, perhaps from North Africa, who we think flourished during the reign of the emperor Hadrian (117–138 C.E.). His one known historical work (its title is unknown) was an abridgment of the Roman wars from the beginning of the Republic to the time of the first emperor, Augustus.

**Frontinus** (ca. 30–104 C.E.) Sextus Iulius Frontinus was a high-ranking Roman senator who served emperors through the end of the first century and the beginning of the second century C.E. He is best known for his service as chief manager of the aqueducts that provided the city of Rome with water and for the technical work that he composed on aqueducts. Frontinus also wrote other technical treatises, including the *Stratagems* (Strategemata), a compilation of various tactical tricks and maneuvers used by military commanders. These examples were taken almost wholly from existing literary and historical texts.

**Livy** (64 B.C.E.–12 C.E.?) The Roman historian Livy (Titus Livius) was born at Patavium (now Padua), in northern Italy, just before the mid-first century B.C.E. During the reign of the first emperor, Augustus, he composed a 142-book *History of Rome* (its Latin title is *Ab Urbe Condita*, "From the founding of the city of Rome") that covered the period from the origins of the city to his own day. Only thirty-five books remain intact. The accounts of the slave wars were in books that have been lost. Only brief *Summaries* (Periochae) of their contents survive. These are of variable quality and provide uneven coverage of the events. For example, they contain information on the first slave war in Sicily and on the Spartacus war, but nothing on the second Sicilian slave war. The writer who was summarizing Livy must have felt that other matters were of greater importance.

**Obsequens, Julius** (late fourth, perhaps early fifth, century C.E.) Julius Obsequens compiled the *Book of Prodigies* (Liber Prodigiorum), which included extraordinary and abnormal occurrences imbued with religious significance. He depended mainly on synopses of the historian Livy, therefore providing us with snippets of information that were originally contained in Livy's lost books.

**Orosius** (ca. 380s–420s C.E.) Paulus Orosius was a Christian priest who fled from Spain to North Africa before the Vandal invasion of Spain in the early fifth century C.E. One of the last historians of the Roman Empire who wrote in Latin, Orosius composed his *History against the Pagans* (Historia adversus paganos) after 415 C.E. at the behest of Saint Augustine. His seven-book history recounts events from the creation of the world to 418 C.E. In regard to the Sicilian slave wars, it is believed that Orosius mainly summarized the accounts by Livy, which have been lost. Orosius's narratives are therefore important because they probably preserve some of Livy's original reports.

**Plutarch** (ca. 40s–120s C.E.) Plutarch was a wealthy landowner and a member of the local aristocracy of the city of Chaeronea, in Greece. Born around the mid-first century C.E., he reached the peak of his political career at the beginning of the second century, in an age when men like himself came to see public service for the Roman Empire as compatible with their traditional Greek culture. The author of numerous and varied works, Plutarch is perhaps most famous for his *Parallel Lives* (Bioi), biographies of eminent Greeks and Romans in which a famous Greek is matched with his equal in the Roman world. For example, Plutarch compared the Athenian politician Pericles with the Roman general Quintus Fabius Maximus.

**Posidonius** (ca. 130s–50s B.C.E.) Posidonius (Poseidonios) was a Stoic philosopher, a historian, and a scientific polymath who originally came from Apamea, in Syria. His fifty-two volume history of the Mediterranean world from 146 B.C.E. to at least the 80s B.C.E. has survived only in fragments. It probably included the principal original accounts of the two great slave wars in Sicily on which Diodorus Siculus depended when he wrote the accounts that we now use as our main sources for information on these wars. For modern scholars, the loss of this history is acute because of the close attention Posidonius paid to social and economic forces in his explanations of historical events.

**Sallust** (ca. 86–35 B.C.E.) The Roman historian Gaius Sallustius Crispus is best known for his history of the Jugurthine War between the Romans and the forces of the African king Jugurtha from 111 to 105 B.C.E., and for his account of the Catiline conspiracy, an unsuccessful revolt against the Roman Republic in 63 B.C.E. In the late 40s and early 30s B.C.E., Sallust also composed an incomplete history of Rome that covered the events from the death of Sulla in 78 B.C.E. at least down to the year 67 B.C.E. Unfortunately, Sallust's *History* (Historiae) has survived only in fragments.

**Seneca** (ca. 1–65 C.E.) Lucius Annaeus Seneca, whose life spanned the first six decades of the first century C.E., was an immensely wealthy Roman senator who came from Spain. He was an important political figure during the reign of the emperor Nero (54–68 C.E.), by whom he was compelled to commit suicide in 65 C.E. Seneca was an adherent of the Stoic school of philosophy and a prolific writer. In some of his moral letters and treatises, he was much concerned with how humans deal with maltreatment and misfortune, a theme also mirrored in his tragedies.

**Strabo** (ca. 60s B.C.E.–20s C.E.) A historian and geographer from Amaseia in Pontus, on the northern shore of modern-day Turkey, and also a student of Stoic philosophy, Strabo composed his main works in the reign of the first Roman emperor, Augustus. His seventeen-book *Geography* (Geôgraphia) covers the whole Mediterranean world under Roman rule. This text has survived in its entirety.

**Suetonius** (ca. 70–130 C.E.) Gaius Suetonius Tranquillus was a distinguished Roman, probably of North African origin, who rose through the imperial service to attain the post of secretary to the emperor Hadrian. He is most famous for his biographies of the rulers of Rome from Julius Caesar to Domitian.

**Tacitus** (ca. 55–120 C.E.?) Cornelius Tacitus was a wellborn Roman senator whose family may have come from southern Gaul. He served in high-ranking imperial posts in the late first and early second centuries C.E. Tacitus is most famous for his two histories of Rome: the *Annals* (Annales), which covers events from 14 to 68 C.E., and the *Histories* (Historiae), which covers the years 69 to 96 C.E.

**Valerius Maximus** (early first century C.E.) Valerius Maximus wrote during the reign of Tiberius, the second emperor of Rome. In the late 20s and early 30s, he compiled a collection titled *Memorable Deeds and Sayings* (Factorum ac dictorum memorabilium libri), featuring famous Romans and non-Romans, which he dedicated to Tiberius. This work is of extremely variable quality, but it preserves items from family sources and traditions that would otherwise be lost.

**Varro** (116–27 B.C.E.) Marcus Terentius Varro came from the town of Reate, about forty-five miles northeast of Rome. As a senator, he was deeply involved in the high politics of his day, but he also was an amazing polymath of Latin culture. As part of the life of leisure that was the cultural obligation and privilege of men of his class, Varro wrote treatises on a wide range of subjects, from satire and biography to music and grammar. In the early 30s B.C.E., when he was eighty years old, he began writing his manual *On Agriculture* (Res Rusticae), a work that he dedicated in part to his wife, Fundania, who had large rural estates of her own. The treatise was both a technical handbook on how to manage a great agricultural estate and a moral guide on how to conduct oneself as an owner. It is worth remembering that Varro would have been in his late teens at the time of the second great slave war in Sicily and that he would have been in his mid-forties at the time of the Spartacus war. Since Varro was an officer who served Pompey throughout this period, including in the war against Sertorius in Spain, it is possible that he had some firsthand experience of the final stages of the Spartacus war.

**Velleius Paterculus** (ca. 20 B.C.E.–30s C.E.?) Gaius Velleius Paterculus was a moderately distinguished Roman senator, soldier, and politician whose professional life spanned the early decades of the first century C.E. He composed a synoptic history under the second Roman emperor, Tiberius. In many respects merely mundane or worse, Velleius's history contains valuable information from historical narratives of the first century B.C.E. that are now lost to us.

# Glossary of Greek and Latin Terms

**aedile**   A Roman magistrate in charge of commerce and the business operations of the state. Aediles issued edicts that governed the sale of slaves in town and city marketplaces.

**as, asses**   A small bronze (later copper) coin in the Roman monetary system; four asses equaled one sestertius.

**cohort**   An operational unit of the Roman army. Ordinarily the major subdivision of the legion, it usually contained about 500 to 550 men.

**consul**   One of the two highest officials of the Roman state, elected annually to a one-year term. The consul's powers could be formally extended, or prorogued, to permit him, as *proconsul*, to exercise the power of a consul in command of military forces in the field or to govern a province of the empire.

**denarius, denarii**   The standard Roman silver coin, worth four sesterces. It was often used as the means of payment of state accounts.

**eques, equites**   Originally, a member of the elite cavalry in the very early Republic. By the period of the slave wars, however, *equites* were essentially wealthy Roman citizens who ranked immediately below senators in prestige and formed a non–office-holding elite. They were often identified with commercial and trading interests, but any clear-cut distinction between them and senators in this regard is misleading. The main difference between them was largely a matter of status and political rank.

**latifundia**   Literally, "wide fields." The term was devised in the early empire to refer to the extensive property holdings of one landlord (*dominus*), which were exploited by a slave workforce. Latifundia were sometimes huge continuous tracts of land, but very often they consisted of a number of farms located in different areas that were held collectively by one *dominus*.

**Latin Name**   Originally, a collection of Latin-speaking communities south of Rome that held a special legal status connecting them to the Roman state. Also, communities of similar status in Italy who were formally tied to the Roman state and who could be called on to provide military assistance.

**legate**   A military officer, appointed by a superior military commander, who acted as the commander's subordinate.

**legion**   The standard unit of the Roman army. Mainly, a large infantry formation, with some additional cavalry, that contained about 5,500 men and was commanded by a consul or his direct subordinate, a praetor.

**lictor**   An attendant of a high-ranking Roman magistrate, usually a consul or praetor, who carried the *fasces*, a ceremonial bundle of bound rods, before the magistrate as a symbol of his power.

**mina**   A unit of money in the eastern part of the Roman Empire that was roughly equal to one hundred denarii.

**ovatio**   A second-rate victory parade awarded to a Roman commander for killing the requisite number of formally recognized enemies of the state. The general walked or rode on horseback and was crowned with myrtle. This procession was much less impressive than a *triumph.*

**pontifex maximus**   The highest ranking priest in the Roman state. He headed the college of *pontifices*, who served on the highest council of priests in Rome. This was a position held for life and was attained by popular election.

**praetor**   A high official of the Roman state, ranking immediately below the consuls in power and authority. He was elected for a one-year term, but his powers could be extended, or *prorogued*, to allow him, as *propraetor*, to command military forces or to govern a province of the empire. There were six praetors at the time of the Sicilian slave wars, eight at the time of the Spartacus war.

**praetorian prefect**   One of the two commanders of the Praetorian Guard at Rome. By the second century C.E., the prefects had achieved a general legal jurisdiction over Italy beyond the one-hundredth milestone outside the city of Rome.

**proconsul**   See *consul.*

**propraetor**   See *praetor.*

**prorogue, prorogation**   To extend in time the powers of a Roman official, such as a consul or praetor. This extension was called a prorogation.

**quaestor**   An official of the Roman state, usually elected for a one-year term and ranking below the praetors and aediles. Normally placed in charge of financial matters, a quaestor could have his powers prorogued and be sent to a province as a fiscal assistant to the Roman governor. There were probably a dozen or more such officials at the time of the Sicilian slave wars, twenty at the time of the Spartacus war.

**senate, senatus consultum**   The senate was the main deliberative body of the Roman state, comprising about three hundred of its most powerful men at the time of the Sicilian slave wars, double that number at the time of the Spartacus war. Senators debated public policy and issued orders to the chief magistrates of the state. Such an order, or piece of advice, was called a *senatus consultum*, which had the effect of law.

**sestertius, sestertii or sesterces**   A bronze coin that was the standard unit of computation in the Roman system of coinage. At the time of the slave wars, four sesterces equaled one denarius.

**Sibylline Books**   A collection of sacred and secret religious texts consulted by the magistrates of the Roman state at the order of the senate whenever an emergency struck.

**talent**   A unit of weight equaling approximately sixty to sixty-five pounds of a precious metal in the eastern Roman Empire. Also, a unit of money. The Attic talent was worth approximately sixty minae or six thousand denarii. In the province of Egypt, however, a talent was worth only about fifteen hundred denarii.

**triumph**   A victory celebration staged by a Roman military commander. It featured a great parade through the city of Rome in which his soldiers marched and the captives and booty taken in the war were put on display,

**vilicus, vilica**   The manager of a farm exploited by slave labor. The vilicus was in charge of all the farm's day-to-day matters, including managing the slaves' work duties and arranging for their food, clothing, and other needs. He was also in charge of acquiring tools and supplies for the farm and reported on the farm's production to the owner, or *dominus*. Frequently, the vilicus himself was a slave or former slave. His wife, the *vilica*, often helped him run the farm.

# A Chronology of the Slave Wars
## (198–60 B.C.E.)

The events of the first and second slave wars on Sicily and of the Spartacus war are highlighted in **boldface.**

| | |
|---|---|
| **198 B.C.E.** | A slave revolt takes place at Setia in Italy. |
| **196 B.C.E.** | The praetor Manius Acilius Glabrio suppresses a slave conspiracy in Etruria. |
| **191 B.C.E.** | The praetor Aulus Cornelius Mammula is sent to Bruttium. |
| **190– 88 B.C.E.** | The praetor (later propraetor) Marcus Tuccius serves in Bruttium and Apulia. |
| **186 B.C.E.** | The Roman senate and the consuls repress a Bacchanalian conspiracy in Rome and southern Italy. |
| **185 B.C.E.** | The praetor Lucius Postumius Tempsanus crushes a slave uprising around Tarentum, in southern Italy. |
| **184 B.C.E.** | The propraetor Lucius Postumius Tempsanus continues the repression of slave uprisings in southern Italy and completes his investigation of Bacchanalian conspiracies in the same region. |
| **183 B.C.E.** | The praetor Lucius Pupius is placed in charge of another inquiry into Bacchanalian conspiracies in southern Italy. |
| **181 B.C.E.** | The praetor Lucius Duronius is put in charge of Apulia and conducts another investigation into Bacchanalian troubles. (*Note:* With the loss of the continuous narrative provided by Livy for the period after 168/67 B.C.E., we are much less well informed about events and government officials to the end of the century.) |
| **160s B.C.E.** | Cato the Elder composes the first extensive manual on slave-based agriculture in Latin. |
| **167 B.C.E.** | The proconsul Lucius Aemilius Paullus, returning to Rome from Macedonia, sacks 70 towns in Epirus and organizes the mass enslavement of about 150,000 people. |

**166 B.C.E.**     Delos, an island in the center of the Aegean Sea, is turned into a free port by the Roman Senate. It becomes a focal point for the slave trade out of the eastern Mediterranean.

**146 B.C.E.**     Rome destroys the cities Carthage and Corinth and enslaves their surviving inhabitants. This marks the end of the first great cycle of Rome's wars of Mediterranean conquest.

**135 B.C.E.**     **Outbreak of the slave war on the island of Sicily, led by Eunus at Enna, in the east-central part of the island. (Lucius?) Cornelius Lentulus, the praetor governing Sicily, is defeated by the rebel slaves. Lucius Plautius Hypsaeus, a praetorian commander on the island, is defeated by the combined slave forces led by Eunus and Kleon.**

**134 B.C.E.**     **The consul Gaius Fulvius Flaccus is assigned to the slave war, superseding Titus Manlius as commander in chief. Manlius is left as a subordinate commander in the central and eastern parts of the island.**

**133 B.C.E.**     **Marcus Perperna defeats rebellious slaves in Sicily and celebrates an ovatio at Rome.**

                   **The praetor Marcus Perperna commands operations against the slaves around Enna. Lucius Calpurnius Piso Frugi, the consular commander, lays siege to Enna. The praetor Titus Manlius conducts operations against slaves in the south-central part of Sicily.**

                   Aristonicus begins a rebellion in Pergamum, in Asia Minor; among his supporters are peasants and slaves.

                   Tiberius Gracchus, tribune of the plebs at Rome, attempts an agrarian reform program but is assassinated.

**132 B.C.E.**     **The consul Publius Rupilius is sent out to conduct the final phases of the war against the slaves in Sicily and to effect a general reorganization of the Roman province.**

**130 B.C.E.**     The revolt of Aristonicus is crushed with the aid of Roman forces under the consul Marcus Perperna.

**123 B.C.E.**     Gaius Gracchus is tribune of the plebs.

**121 B.C.E.**     Gaius Gracchus is assassinated.

**105 B.C.E.**     The war against King Jugurtha in North Africa ends. The consul Gaius Marius now directs the principal Roman military efforts against large-scale Germanic invasions in southern Gaul.

**104 B.C.E.**     **Publius Licinius Nerva, the praetor governing Sicily, receives an order from the senate to investigate the status of free persons illegally held in slavery on the island. The second Sicilian slave war, led by Salvius (a.k.a. Tryphon) and Athenion, begins.**

Lucius Licinius Lucullus, one of the praetors at Rome, receives a command against rebel slaves at Capua, in southern Italy.

**103 B.C.E.**  **Lucius Licinius Lucullus, as propraetor, takes command of the war against the slaves in Sicily.**

**102 B.C.E.**  **Salvius (Tryphon) dies. Athenion takes over the leadership of the slave forces in Sicily. Gaius Servilius, as propraetor, takes command of the Roman forces.**

The praetor Marcus Antonius takes command of Roman forces against the Cilician pirates. During his fourth consulship, Gaius Marius defeats the Teutones and Ambrones in the Battle of Aquae Sextiae.

**101 B.C.E.**  **The consul Manius Aquillius is dispatched to fight the slaves in Sicily.**

During his fifth consulship, Gaius Marius defeats the Cimbri in the Battle of Vercellae, in northern Italy. Marcus Antonius, as proconsul, continues his command against the pirates.

**100 B.C.E.**  **Roman forces under the command of Manius Aquillius, as proconsul, bring an end to the second slave war in Sicily.**

**99 B.C.E.**  Manius Aquillius returns to Rome to celebrate an *ovatio* for his victory in Sicily.

**91–**

**88 B.C.E.**  Rome and its Italian allies fight the Italian War.

**86 B.C.E.**  Gaius Marius dies.

**83–**

**82 B.C.E.**  Civil war in Italy rages between the supporters of Sulla and those of Gaius Marius's political heirs.

**82–**

**79 B.C.E.**  The domination of Lucius Cornelius Sulla as dictator (82–81 B.C.E.).

**78 B.C.E.**  Sulla dies.

**77 B.C.E.**  Renewed civil war in Italy; insurrection of the proconsul Marcus Aemilius Lepidus.

**77–**

**72 B.C.E.**  The Roman central state wages war against the renegade Quintus Sertorius in Spain. Pompey the Great is dispatched to command the Roman forces, which finally brings the war to an end by a covert operation. Sertorius is assassinated.

**73 B.C.E.**    **Gladiators under the leadership of Spartacus break out from the gladiatorial training school at Capua, beginning the Spartacus slave war. The praetor Gaius Claudius Glaber is unsuccessful in his attempt to besiege the slaves on Vesuvius. Lucius Cossinius, sent out to assist the praetor Publius Varinius, is almost captured in battle and dies.**

Gaius Verres serves his first year as governor of the province of Sicily.

**72 B.C.E.**    **Armies sent out against the slaves and commanded by the two consuls, Lucius Gellius Publicola and Gnaeus Cornelius Lentulus Clodianus, are defeated by Spartacus. Quintus Arrius, as propraetor, scores a great victory over the slaves led by Crixus in Apulia, but he and Gellius are later defeated by Spartacus. Marcus Licinius Crassus acquires overall command of the war against Spartacus. The praetor Gnaeus Manlius is defeated by Spartacus.**

Gaius Verres serves his second year as governor of Sicily.

**71 B.C.E.**    **The Roman army, under the proconsul Marcus Licinius Crassus, temporarily traps Spartacus in Bruttium during the winter, but Spartacus escapes. The final battle against the slaves takes place in northern Lucania. Roman legions under the proconsul Pompey the Great arrive from Spain to confront the remnants of the slave forces; six thousand slaves are crucified along the Appian Way.**

Gaius Verres serves his third and final year as governor of Sicily.

**70 B.C.E.**    Pompey the Great and Marcus Licinius Crassus serve as consuls.

Cicero leads the prosecution of Gaius Verres, former governor of Sicily.

**70–**
**60 B.C.E.**    Mopping-up operation against fugitive slaves in southern Italy.

**67 B.C.E.**    Pompey the Great receives an extensive military command to rid the Mediterranean of piracy.

**63 B.C.E.**    The conspiracy of the young Roman nobleman Lucius Sergius Catilina (Catiline). There are fears that slaves will become involved in the armed insurrection when the fighting breaks out, but Catiline refuses to recruit them.

**61 B.C.E.**    Gaius Octavius involved in mopping up operations against remnants of Spartacus's and Catiline's followers in Southern Italy.

# Questions for Consideration

1. What similarities can you see in the three major slave wars? To what extent do you think that Spartacus and the slaves who rebelled with him were repeating earlier patterns of slave rebellion? In what ways was the Spartacus war different from the earlier slave wars and why?

2. What is the relationship between the more usual forms of slave resistance (running away, stealing, deliberately damaging tools and property, doing harm to one's master) and the types of resistance found in the slave wars?

3. What factors created the social and economic conditions favoring large scale armed resistance to servitude? To what extent do you think the slaveholders were aware of these factors?

4. How do the historical sources on the Spartacus war differ among themselves? How does the character of the surviving evidence determine how historians view the events? Does the fact that some of the accounts were written close in time to the events themselves and others centuries later affect the way in which historians use them? Is there any distinction in value because some authors, such as Plutarch, were biographers, whereas others, such as Sallust, were historians?

5. Were the slave owners conscious of potential resistance? What means did they use to control their slaves so as to prevent resistance to their control? What slave activities did they perceive as particularly threatening and dangerous? Were they right? Were these proclivities among the slaves apparent in the wars?

6. What was the role of religion in the mobilization of the slaves in southern Italy and Sicily between the end of the Hannibalic War (201 B.C.E.) and the Spartacus slave war (73–71 B.C.E.)? Were there any similarities in the types of religion involved? Was the role of religion the same as, or different from, the religious factor in modern slave rebellions?

7. Leadership is usually a very important factor for any collective armed slave resistance. What were some of the characteristics of the commanders of the rebel slaves that made them successful leaders?

8. Although no words or accounts of the slaves themselves have survived, is it possible to reconstruct what some of their motives or aims were?

What do you think were the objectives they hoped to achieve when they rebelled?

9. Did the slaves succeed? What does successful resistance in the case of slaves mean? What significance would you, as a historian, give to large-scale violent resistance to slavery as seen in these wars? In the history of slavery? In the history of human freedom? In our understanding of how slave societies actually worked?

10. If the slave rebellions ultimately failed, then what were the main reasons leading to their lack of success? Was there anything that the slaves could have done differently that would have produced a more favorable result for them?

11. The wars pitted former slaves on the one side against free persons, represented by the magistrates of the state, on the other. By reading carefully, can you discern the participation of other free persons (peasant farmers or poor citizens, for example) in these wars? Did they play a significant role?

# Selected Bibliography

GENERAL RESOURCES

Wiedemann, Thomas. *Greek and Roman Slavery: A Sourcebook.* Baltimore: Johns Hopkins University Press, 1981; New York: Routledge, 1991.

SLAVES AND SLAVERY

Bradley, Keith R. *Slaves and Masters in the Roman Empire: A Study in Social Control.* Oxford: Oxford University Press, 1984, esp. chap. 1, "Loyalty and Obedience," 21–45; and chap. 4, "Fear, Abuse, Violence," 113–37.
_____. *Slavery and Society at Rome.* Cambridge: Cambridge University Press, 1994, esp. chap. 6, "Resisting Slavery," 107–31.
Hopkins, Keith. *Conquerors and Slaves.* Cambridge: Cambridge University Press, 1978.
Watson, Alan. *Roman Slave Law.* Baltimore: Johns Hopkins University Press, 1987, esp. chap. 8, "Punishment of the Slave," 115–33.
Wiedemann, Thomas. *Slavery.* New Surveys in the Classics, no. 19. Oxford: Clarendon Press, 1987, esp. chap. 6, "Discontent and Rebellion," 47–51.

SLAVE RESISTANCE

Fuks, Alexander. "Slave War and Slave Troubles in Chios in the Third Century B.C." *Athenaeum* 46 (1968): 102–11. Reprinted in *Social Conflict in Ancient Greece*, 260–69. Jerusalem, 1984.

FUGITIVES AND RUNAWAYS

Jones, Christopher P. "*Stigma:* Tattooing and Branding in Graeco-Roman Antiquity." *Journal of Roman Studies* 77 (1987): 139–55.
Llewelyn, Stephen R. "The Government's Pursuit of Runaway Slaves." Chap. 3 in *New Documents Illustrating Early Christianity*, edited by S. R. Lewelyn, Grand Rapids, 1998. 18:9–46.
Thurmond, D. L. "Some Roman Slave Collars in *CIL.*" *Athenaeum* 82 (1994): 459–93.

**SLAVE WARS: GENERAL**

Bradley, Keith R. *Slavery and Rebellion in the Roman World, 140 B.C.–70 B.C.* Bloomington: Indiana University Press, 1989.

Toynbee, Arnold J. "The Insurrections of Slaves in the Post-Hannibalic Age." Chap. 9 in *Hannibal's Legacy*, 2:313–31. Oxford, 1965.

Urbainczyk, Theresa. *Slave Revolts in Antiquity*. Berkeley: University of California Press, 2008.

Vogt, Joseph. "The Structure of Ancient Slave Wars." Chap. 3 in *Ancient Slavery and the Ideal of Man*, 39–92. Oxford, 1974.

**THE SICILIAN SLAVE WARS**

Bradley, Keith R. "Slave Kingdoms in Ancient Sicily." *Historical Reflections/ Réflexions historiques* 10 (1983): 435–51.

Finley, M. I. "The Great Slave Revolts." Chap. 11 in *Ancient Sicily to the Arab Conquest*, 137–47. London, 1968; London: Chatto & Windus, 1979.

Forrest, W. G. G., and T. C. W. Stinton. "The First Sicilian Slave War." *Past and Present* 21 (1962): 87–93.

Green, Peter. "The First Sicilian Slave War." *Past and Present* 20 (1961): 10–29.

Rubinsohn, Wolfgang Zeev. "Some Remarks on the Causes and Repercussions of the So-Called 'Second Slave Revolt' in Sicily." *Athenaeum* 60 (1982): 436–51.

Strasburger, Herman. "Poseidonios on Problems of the Roman Empire." *Journal of Roman Studies* 55 (1965): 40–53.

Verbrugghe, Gerald P. "Slave Rebellion or Sicily in Revolt?" *Kokalos* 20 (1974): 46–60.

**GLADIATORS AND SLAVERY**

Grant, Michael. *Gladiators*. London: Wiedenfeld & Nicolson, 1967.

Hopkins, Keith. "Murderous Games." Chap. 1 in *Death and Renewal: Sociological Studies in Roman History* 2:1–30. Cambridge, 1983.

Wiedemann, Thomas. *Emperors and Gladiators*. New York: Routledge, 1992.

**THE SPARTACUS WAR**

In addition to the specific studies noted below, three more recent general studies of the Spartacus slave war should be noted:

Schiavone, Aldo. *Spartacus*. Cambridge, Mass.: Harvard University Press, 2013 [trans. J. Carden, of: *Spartaco: le armi e l'uomo*, Turin, 2011].

Strauss, Barry. *The Spartacus War*. New York: Simon & Schuster, 2009.

Urbainczyk, Theresa. *Spartacus*. London: Bristol Classical Press, 2004.

Bodor, Alexandr. "The Ethnic and Social Composition of the Participants in the Slave Uprising Led by Spartacus." In *Spartacus: Symposium Rebus*

*Spartaci Gestis Dedicatum 2050A*, edited by C. M. Danov and A. Fol, 85–94. Sofia, 1981.

Doi, Masaoki. "On the Negotiations between the Roman State and the Spartacus Army." *Klio* 66 (1984): 170–74.

———. "The Present Stage of Studies on Spartacus' Uprising and Its Problems." *Studies in Humanities* 35 (1985): 17–45.

———. *A Bibliography of [the] Bellum Spartacium.* Tokyo, 1989.

———. "Female Slaves in Spartacus' Army." In M. M. Mactoux and G. Evelyne, eds. *Mélanges Pierre Lévêque.* Paris: Les Belles Lettres (1989): 161–72.

———. "The Origins of Spartacus and the Anti-Roman Struggle in Thracia." *Index* 20 (1992): 31–40.

Rubinsohn, Wolfgang Zeev. "Was the *Bellum Spartacium* a Slave Insurrection?" *Rivista di Filologia e di Istruzione Classica* 99 (1971): 290–99.

## COMPARATIVE WORKS ON MODERN SLAVE WARS AND REBELLIONS

The literature on this subject is vast. The titles suggested below are only some of the recommended works. If you wish to acquire more detailed references, consult Joseph C. Miller, ed., *Slavery and Slaving in World History: A Bibliography, 1900–1991* (Millwood, N.Y.: Krauss International, 1993), under the index headings "fugitives," "resistance," and "revolts." Also see Seymour Drescher and Stanley L. Engerman, eds., *A Historical Guide to World Slavery* (New York, 1998), which provides many useful entries on basic thematic areas of slavery, including rebellion and resistance. Junius P. Rodriguez, ed., *The Historical Encyclopedia of World Slavery.* 2 vols. (Santa Barbara, ABC-Clio, 1997) is similarly useful as a basic reference for many of the aspects of slavery pertinent to the Spartacus war. Especially relevant as a general source work is the first volume of the *Cambridge World History of Slavery,* edited by Keith Bradley and Paul Cartledge, published in 2011; it contains numerous entries useful to an understanding of slave resistance and rebellion in the ancient world. The best resource on resistance is James C. Scott, *Domination and the Arts of Resistance: Hidden Transcripts* (New Haven, Conn.: Yale University Press, 1990), which is in a class by itself.

Campbell, Stanley W. *The Slave Catchers: Enforcement of the Fugitive Slave Law, 1850–1860.* New York: Norton, 1968.

Craton, Michael. *Testing the Chains: Resistance to Slavery in the British West Indies.* Ithaca, N.Y.: Cornell University Press, 1982.

da Costa, Emilia Viotti. *Crowns of Glory, Tears of Blood: The Demarara Slave Rebellion of 1823.* New York: Oxford University Press, 1994. This is perhaps the best single study of a large-scale New World slave rebellion.

Davis, David Brion. "A Black Slave Revolt in the Fertile Crescent." Chap. 1 in *Slavery and Human Progress* 5–8. New York: Oxford University Press, 1984.

Franklin, John Hope, and Loren Schweninger. *Runaway Slaves: Rebels on the Plantations, 1790–1860.* New York: Oxford University Press, 1999.

Genovese, Eugene D. *From Rebellion to Revolution: Afro-American Slave Revolts in the Making of the Modern World.* Baton Rouge: Louisiana State University Press, 1979. Also see the review by Winthrop D. Jordan, "Why Didn't Slaves Rebel?" *New York Review of Books* 27, no. 6 (April 17, 1980): 18–19.

Heuman, Gad. *"The Killing Time": The Morant Bay Rebellion in Jamaica.* London: Macmillan, 1994.

_____, ed. *Out of the House of Bondage: Runaways, Resistance, and Marronage in Africa and the New World.* London: Frank Cass, 1986.

James, C. L. R. *The Black Jacobins: Toussaint l'Ouverture and the San Domingo Revolution.* 2nd rev. ed. New York: Random House, 1963.

Klein, Herbert S. "Slave Resistance and Rebellion." Chap. 9 in *African Slavery in Latin America and the Caribbean,* 189–215. New York: Oxford University Press, 1986.

Mullin, Gerald W. *Flight and Rebellion: Slave Resistance in Eighteenth-Century Virginia.* New York: Oxford University Press, 1972.

Popovic, Alexandre. *The Revolt of the African Slaves in Iraq,* translated by Léon King. Princeton, N.J.: Markus Wiener, 1999.

Price, Richard. *Alabi's World.* Baltimore: Johns Hopkins University Press, 1990. Also see the review by E. J. Hobsbawm, "Escaped Slaves of the Forest." *New York Review of Books* 37, no. 19 (December 6, 1990): 46–48.

_____, ed. *Maroon Societies: Rebel Slave Communities in the Americas.* Rev. ed. Baltimore: Johns Hopkins University Press, 1979.

Reis, João José. *Slave Rebellion in Brazil: The Muslim Uprisings of 1835 in Bahia.* Trans. A. Brakel. Baltimore-London: The Johns Hopkins University Press, 1995.

## SPARTACUS IN HISTORICAL WRITING

Griffith, John G. "Spartacus and the Growth of Historical and Political Legends." In *Spartacus: Symposium Rebus Spartaci Gestis dedicatum 2050A,* edited by C. M. Danov and A. Fol, 65–70. Sophia, 1981.

Korzheva, K. P. "Spartacus' Rebellion in Soviet Historiography." *Soviet Studies in History* 15, no. 1 (Summer 1976): 67–97.

Rubinsohn, Wolfgang Zeev. *Spartacus' Uprising and Soviet Historical Writing,* translated by John G. Griffith. Oxford: Oxbow Books, 1987.

## SPARTACUS IN FICTION

Fast, Howard. *Spartacus.* New York: Planetarium Station, 1951; New York: Crown, 1958; New York: Bantam, 1960; Armonk, N.Y.: North Castle Books, 1997.

Koestler, Arthur. *The Gladiators,* translated by Edith Simon. London: Jonathan Cape, 1939; 2nd ed., New York: Graphic Books, 1956; New York: Bantam Books, 1962; with new postscript, New York: Macmillan, 1965.

ON THE AUTHORS

Fast, Howard. *Being Red.* Boston: Houghton Mifflin, 1990, esp. chap. 14.

Koestler, Arthur. "Excursion in the First Century B.C." Chap. 24 in *The Invisible Writing,* 261–68. Yol. 2 of *Arrow in the Blue.* New York, 1954.

FILMS AND TELEVISION

From 1911 to the present, there have been at least five major feature films on Spartacus, including Italian (1913) and Russian (1967) ones, but the most famous and influential film is the Hollywood epic produced by Kirk Douglas and released in 1960. Cinematic and television versions of the Spartacus revolt continue to be made, beginning with the made-for-television movie *Spartacus* (2004): 174 minutes, directed by Robert Dornhelm and staring Goren Visnjic as Spartacus; the teleplay by Robert Schenkkan is based on Howard Fast's novel. Starz channel produced a made-for-television miniseries (2010), thirteen episodes filmed in New Zealand: *Spartacus: Blood and Sand,* starring Andy Whitfield as Spartacus; three series followed: a six-part "prequel" *Spartacus: Gods of the Arena* (2011); followed by *Spartacus: Vengeance* (2011) and *Spartacus: War of the Damned* (2013), all starring Liam McIntyre as Spartacus.

*Spartacus.* Bryna Films/Universal Pictures, 1960, 197 min.; reedited version, restoration by Robert A. Harris and James C. Katz, 1991, 198 min. Screenplay: Dalton Trumbo, based on the novel by Howard Fast. Director: Stanley Kubrick. Musical score: Alex North. Cast: Kirk Douglas (Spartacus); Sir Laurence Olivier (Marcus Licinius Crassus); Jean Simmons (Varinia, Spartacus's wife); Sir Charles Laughton (Lentulus Gracchus); Peter Ustinov (Lentulus Batiatus); Tony Curtis (Antoninus); John Gavin (Julius Caesar); Woody Strode (Draba).

On the film and its historical context, see Maria Wyke, "Spartacus: Testing the Strength of the Body Politic," chap. 3 in *Projecting the Past: Ancient Rome, Cinema, and History,* 34–72 (New York: Routledge, 1997); and Natalie Zemon Davis, "Resistance and Survival: Spartacus," chap. 2 in *Slaves on Screen: Film and Historical Vision* (Cambridge, Mass.: Harvard University Press, 2000), 17–40. In general on the making of the film and its background, one can consult the studies collected by Martin M. Winkler, ed., *Spartacus: Film and History* (Malden, Mass.: Blackwell, 2007), and, more tangentially, his *Gladiator: Film and History* (Malden, Mass.: Blackwell, 2004). I would also like to recommend the doctoral dissertation by Fiona Radford, "The Many Legends of Spartacus: The Production History of a Film" (PhD dissertation, Sydney, Macquarie University, 2012), a work that I hope will see publication in the near future. New television adaptations include *Spartacus,* TV movie, 2004: 2 hours 54 minutes; director: Robert Dornhelm and starring Goren Visnjic as Spartacus, teleplay Robert Schenkkan (based on Howard Fast's novel); and the Starz American TV miniseries in 2010 (filmed in New

Zealand), thirteen episodes: *Spartacus: Blood and Sand*, starring Andy Whitfield as Spartacus; *Spartacus: Gods of the Arena* (six-part prequel, in 2011); *Spartacus: Vengeance* (third series in 2011); *Spartacus: War of the Damned* (fourth series, 2013): Liam McIntyre as Spartacus in series 2–4.

MUSIC AND DANCE

*Spartacus.* Musical score: Aram Khachaturian (1956; rev., 1960). Choreography Leonid Jakobson (1956); Igor Moiseyev (1958); Yuri Grigorovitch (1968). Perhaps best appreciated in the musical highlights of the ballet in a performance by the London Symphony Orchestra, dir. Aram Khachaturian. EMI, 1977; digitally remastered, Abbey Road, 1988, CD-EMX-2119.

Ballet: Vasiliev, Vladimir. *Spartacus.* Bolshoi Ballet, with the Orchestra of the Bolshoi Theater, 1977. Musical score: Aram Khachaturian. Choreography: Yuri Grigorovitch. Screenplay and photography: Y. Grigorovitch and V. Derbenev. Corinth Films, 1988, 95 min.; and a full-length version (128 min.) again by the Bolshoi Ballet (HBO Video, 1984).

# Index